Creating Reality

HOW TV NEWS
DISTORTS EVENTS

Creating Reality

HOW TV NEWS
DISTORTS EVENTS

David L. Altheide

A SageMark Edition

SAGE PUBLICATIONS   Beverly Hills   London

Originally published as Volume 33, Sage Library of Social Research.

Copyright © 1974 by Sage Publications, Inc.

For information address:

SAGE PUBLICATIONS, INC.
275 South Beverly Drive
Beverly Hills, California 90212

SAGE PUBLICATIONS LTD
28 Banner Street
London EC1Y 8QE, England

Printed in the United States of America

International Standard Book Number 0-8039-0846-6

Library of Congress Catalog Card No. 76-22602

THIRD SAGEMARK PRINTING—MAY 1977

CONTENTS

INTRODUCTION

With the publication of this book, Professor David Altheide joins a small group of social analysts such as Fred W. Friendly, Edward J. Epstein, and Gaye Tuchman who have investigated the inner workings and the social and political implications of television's newsmaking machinery. However, his work, "Creating Reality: How TV News Distorts Events," while focusing primarily on television newsmaking, is also an interpretation of the social and political functions of the craft of journalism in modern society. In the latter respect, this work follows in the tradition of mass media analysis begun by Walter Lippmann in 1922 in his book *Public Opinion,* and continued in his later study *The Phantom Public.* This work follows the sociological tradition of news analysis in a direct line from the work of Robert E. Park and Helen MacGill Hughes.

Since the virtues of this book are closely related to Professor Altheide's craftsmanship as a researcher, a few words about how his study came about will help the reader understand its importance. The project began in 1971 as a study of a network affiliate's newsroom. While doing his research at the level of the local community, he developed his conception of "the news perspective," by which he means the complex of economic, organizational, and personal factors that determine the baises and the slants built into news reporting. He saw in concrete detail how the interaction between politicians, businessmen, political activists, and the newsroom staff influenced the selection and treatment of news. He also saw a heightened awareness on the part of almost all groups of their potential capacity to influence the direction of new bias in their own favor. Politically oriented groups have absorbed and mastered to a surprising degree not only television technology but the methods for the production and distribution of television images.

Although Altheide made his basic discoveries while studying a specific newsroom, these discoveries forced him to expand the scope of his observations in order to include the role of the networks in relations with their affiliates. He thus expanded his research to include stations in Washington, California, and Arizona. As a result he added to his worms-eye view, acquired at the local level, the perspective of the central managers of the American newsmaking industry. His understanding of the vertical structure of the industry opened his eyes to the nationwide processes of the manufacture and marketing of news images.

Luckily for us, Professor Altheide was in the midst of his research enterprise during the presidential campaigns of 1972. Not since 1952, when television first reported political party conventions, had journalism played so dramatic a political role as it did in 1972. The period between July of 1972 and August of 1974 embraced Watergate, the resignation of the Democratic Party's vice presidential nominee, Senator Eagleton, and the forced resignation of President Nixon. Altheide was prepared for these events and absorbed them into his research. His analysis of them brings us to the frontier of our knowledge about the relationship between print and television journalism and their combined role in politics.

By responding to the issues that were presented to him while carrying out his investigation and by making them part of his problem, he has seen, as few others have, the complexity of the struggle for the manufacture and appropriation of images among competing political groups.

Since the election campaigns of 1972, and especially since the Kennedy-Nixon television debates in 1960, the political uses of television have become vastly more sophisticated. An entirely new set of institutions and specialists have been developed for the purpose of organizing the production and distribution of preferred political images. Television has become an integral part of the political process, and specialists in the arts of image management have become important gatekeepers between the politician and the citizen. Like the journalist before him, the television newsman has become a professional at politics; yet, also like the journalist, he does not have a recognized status as such.

Democracy has been based on the premise that the citizen is capable of political judgment and that he or she will express this political judgment when voting for those who are to be the citizen's representatives. However, professional politicians in democracies typically have not trusted the political judgment of voters and have traditionally sought ways to aid voters in making their choices. Thus, party bosses and party machinery have had as their role the organized management of citizens' voting behavior. The political parties of democracies are composed of a small group of leaders whose primary business is to run the party and a large number of party members who are activated at the time of elections to vote for candidates who have been selected by party bosses. So long as party bosses can control the party organization, the mass of passive citizens have not been a threat to the organized management of politics in the democracies, and the democracies have not been threatened by control of politics by amateurs.

It is a peculiarity of the American democracy that its president is chosen in a popular election held once every four years. This has been called plebescitary democracy, wherein the president, once elected, is not necessarily committed to either his party's platform or to his party organization. His power is believed to derive directly from having received a mandate from the people, not from the party. In European democracies, by contrast, the leader received his mandate from his party and may be removed by his party without recourse to either impeachment or a nationwide popular election. But in receiving his mandate directly from the people in a national plebescite, an American president then rules on the strength of his popular legitimation, and while his power is regarded to be somehow proportionate to the size of his popular plurality of votes, he can rule without regard to the daily vicissitudes of public or party opinion.

Between elections, the party regulars in the local communities and in the state organizations hold political jobs, receive and distribute patronage, and stand ready to activate party regulars whose services will be necessary to organize the voters during the next election. The stock in trade of the political boss has been his ability to deliver votes for the party, and, accordingly, he has been

rewarded when he does so successfully. George Washington Plunkitt described and defended this party system at the turn of the
century. He fought the civil service reformers because they would
deprive him of the sources of patronage that were the basis of his
capacity to bring out the vote for the party.[1]

Party bosses have always fought against all tendencies that
would democratize the political process by giving the citizen a
political role. In presidential elections, that role has been restricted
to voting in primary elections and to voting in the presidential
election in November. Despite some recent changes in party rules
—especially in the Democratic Party—designed to commit delegates to specific candidates, party bosses are still the political
brokers in the negotiating process that leads to candidate selection. When they have been deprived of this role, as was the case
in the selection of George McGovern as the presidential candidate
of the Democratic Party in 1972, the bosses do not regard themselves as having a commitment to the candidate, because the candidate has none to them. McGovern discovered what happens when
the voters are allowed to make their own choices; namely, that,
having captured the convention, he had lost the party's backing.
Ultimately, he could win only in Massachusetts, where the party
organization, prodded by Senator Kennedy, supported him and
turned out the vote.

The efforts of the party bosses to retain control over the selection of presidential candidates have faced a new threat from television, for television grants to the candidate the possibility for vast
public exposure and accentuates the element of the popularity
contest. When a candidate captures the public imagination, it is
immeasurably more difficult for the bosses within the party to
oppose him openly. Thus television may be used by candidates
to restrict the bosses' areas of choice, as in the example of George
McGovern. But, of course, the political bosses have also learned
to use television to accomplish their own objectives. Hence, television has been absorbed into the political process and has been
made a tool of party politics as well.

More than any of their political predecessors, Richard Nixon
and his men understood the technology of television in relation
to politics. No doubt it was partly Nixon's hostile relationship to
political journalists that forced him to devote his attention to this

problem, but he also understood, as an incumbent president, that he could use television to free himself from control by the party machinery. He set up the Committee to Re-elect the President, and used it as a vehicle to circumvent his dependency on the party for money, and as an agency through which he could present himself to the people directly. Since he was able to bypass the party, he owed nothing to it after the election. As Professor Altheide shows, the entire reelection campaign was based on a mastery of television, including not only the timing of political announcements to gain maximum exposure, but the organizing of the Republican nominating convention so that the networks had almost no choice but to present President Nixon to the public on his own terms. The affiliates had the options of aping the networks or scrounging for news angles that would have a local or regional appeal—e.g., human interest stories about convention delegates. In that campaign, television played a role similar to the mass rally as an instrument of demagogic politics.

The convention and the campaign were also illustrations of the defeat of the party bosses by the direct democratization of the presidential election. Thus, political television, in the hands of those who can master it, vastly enhances the possibilities for demagogic political power in the American democracy, for it can eliminate the pluralism inherent in the boss system.

It is not yet clear to what extent television newsmaking has become editorially tied to the political opinions of network and affiliate owners and managers. According to Altheide, the Eagleton story was largely a product of the fact that it occurred in August, when there was otherwise a short supply of news. In his study of the making of that story, he was unable to find any forces at work other than the insatiability of the news media for the raw materials needed to produce an endless succession of dramatic human interest reports. The competition for Nielsen ratings seems to have priority as a standard of selection in news reporting. It appears, at least up to now, that politically explicit tastes and preferences on the part of owners and managers are secondary to the immediate economics of advertising rates and the income they produce.

The amount of time that the networks and their affiliates devote to news has been increasing continuously since 1950. One reason for this is that news programs have been popular with the public. Another reason is that the Federal Communications Commission has steadily increased the amount of time that must be devoted to public affairs programming. Currently, fifteen percent of all programming must be devoted to news and public affairs. The increase in the amount of time devoted to news programming has been paralleled by an increase in the pressure to attract and hold audiences. As a result, the format of news reporting has become much more complex and expensive, and the total investment in news programs has increased, prices for commercials have risen, and the need for advertisers has intensified. Inevitably, these commercial pressures have acted to suppress controversy in news reporting and to encourage editorial neutrality: the assumption behind the so-called editorial reply which supplies equal time to opposing viewpoints is that one viewpoint cancels its opposite. But the major effect of increased economic pressure on news programs has been a massive tendency to personalize the news format and to stress the human interest dimensions of news stories. In direct ratio as newsmen and women have become friendly figures in our living rooms sharing their own private lives with us, they present to us in increasingly intimate terms the private lives of the people who are the subjects of the news. In the days of the tabloid, this was known as 'yellow journalism,' and it can still be regarded as such. Now, however, it is not only the lower masses who may take vicarious pleasure from the troubles of others. The middle classes have become major consumers of such journalism and the upper classes employ press agents to gain them the exposure they feel is their due. The news media have discovered that the philandering of ex-presidents, the psychiatric history of vice presidential candidates, and the skeletons in the closets of celebrities are marketable to all classes. The adaptation of yellow journalism by television seems to be one of its major contributions to American civilization.

While television news turns increasingly to human interest stories and yellow journalism in order to hold its audiences, it has not been able to clarify for itself its role in American politics. Its political impact—as shown in the Eagleton and Nixon resignations —can be great, but the political role it has played has not been based on an effort to achieve explicit political objectives. Instead of formulating its own political objectives, it has attempted to formulate an ideology of "disinterested objectivity," implying that "this is the way it is," or "we present the news from nobody's point of view." Ideologies which stress neutrality do not provide specific guidelines for either selection or presentation of news. Claims to objectivity and neutrality are an admission of an absence of editorial policy in the area of politics.

One result of this situation is that each television newsroom uses as its basis for selection of news the judgments of newsmanagers in other newsrooms; newsmanagers solve their own problems of selection by emulating the selections of their competitors. This mutual emulation by competitors results in a remarkable degree of sameness between the news programs of the networks. When this practice is applied to news stories with a political content, it has the effect of reinforcing the importance of the event so selected. It is in this sense that news images presented by television can become a reality in their own right without their having been willed so by the political orientation of the networks.

If it is true that the political impact of television is a result of the accumulation of the unplanned, mutually reinforced, individual actions of competitors for the attention of mass audiences, the managers of television news cannot be accused of political bias in a formal sense. The bias that results is rather the bias of political irresponsibility, an unwillingness to be political in any sense that might prejudice ratings.

Television's political news does indeed play an ambiguous role in American society. On the one hand, it can be manipulated by those politicians who understand its ways and who have clearly defined their own political objectives. On the other hand, it contributes to political sensationalism and to the growing skepticism of the public in regard to their leaders and their political institutions. Thus, while television has vastly increased the circus aspect of American politics without in any way raising or lowering the levels of political ignorance of the public, it has also scrupulously refrained from assuming any responsibility for the results it produces.

One of the passions that underlies Professor Altheide's work is his hope that his book will contribute to increasing the public's awareness of the sources and content of television's new bias. His hope is that the informed citizen will learn to supply the intellectual compensations necessary to restoring reality to the distorted images presented to us by television. While he sees television as a rotten egg that is growing bigger and bigger, his conclusion places the full burden of intellectual and political responsibility on the individual citizen. We can hope with Professor Altheide that his faith in the heroic citizen will be fulfilled, but it remains to be seen which will prevail, the responsible citizen or the irresponsible news media. The future of American democracy as we know it may well depend on this uneven match.

Arthur J. Vidich
New School for Social Research

NOTE

1. *Plunkitt of Tammany Hall; A Series of Very Plain Talks on Very Practical Politics* by William L. Riordon, E. P. Dutton and Co., N.Y. 1963.

PREFACE

This is a study of television news. A three-year research project, including more than one year in a network affiliate station, provided the materials for my assessment of current news practices. While the focus is on TV news, it will be clear that many of the points I make can also be applied to print journalism. My aim is to clarify how the news process works in order to improve certain inadequacies. I believe that nightly newscasts are distorting what they claim to represent, and in the process are adding to our social problems. Journalism is too important in our society for these practices to continue.

The first step is to be aware of how newsworkers look at the world and do their work. This is especially important for news watchers who must learn to evaluate the nightly news reports if they are not to be misled. In the pages that follow, I argue that the organization of news for practical reasons encourages the adaptation of a convoluted way of simplifying events. I call this outlook the *news perspective.* I trace the foundations of this powerful bias through commercialism, scheduling, technology, and competition. Ethnographic materials show how these constraints are filtered into the daily affairs of news personnel. The impact of this institutionalized way of looking at the world is shown in specific local and national stories. I then offer partial solutions to this crucial problem and suggest ways to defensively scrutinize news messages in order to understand how the news process has shaped them.

This project began as a study of a network affiliate's newsroom in 1971. By the time that study was completed in 1974, the focus had broadened to include other aspects of news. This led me to further investigate major stories like Watergate, as well as expand my sample of stations to include others in Washington state, California, and Arizona. My involvements with dozens of news personnel in these settings forged research commitments to protect their anonymity. Pseudonyms are used for some cities, such as Western City, and specific stations, such as Channels A and B.

I am very grateful to the network and affiliate employees who helped me become less naive about their craft. This is especially true of my friends at Channel B who tolerated my questions and mistakes until I could become a little more like them. The research at Channel B was partially supported by a National Institute of Health Fellowship (5 f01 MH 54729), and several community colleges which provided employment during 1971-1973.

Other people provided intellectual and human support during this project. Jack D. Douglas gave a model of scholarship and commitment to sociology. Stanford M. Lyman, Joseph R. Gusfield, and Virgil J. Olson helped me reach for the sociological imagination. My brother, Duane, gave me encouragement by believing in my work. John Bradford read drafts of this manuscript and offered suggestions. Paul Rasmussen's study of Channel A, and our extended conversations, helped me understand more about Channel B. Kerry Teeple made much of this work possible by helping me gain access to the newsroom and by patiently explaining what I did not understand. Robert Gilmore provided information about several news reports as well as unselfish friendship. Robert Snow is thanked for encouraging our ongoing dialogue about the significance of media in our lives. John Johnson was especially helpful and supportive of this work. Suzanne Johnson and Kathy Rasmussen also contributed more than they know. But my greatest gratitude goes to my wife, Carla, who shared in it all and gave us two lovely children in the process. This book is for her, with my love.

Chapter 1

TV NEWS AND EVERYDAY LIFE

Americans like news. Every day 65 million Americans watch the news on one of the three major television networks. Even more viewers watch an additional half-hour or more of local TV news, produced by nearly 600 stations affiliated with the networks and a number of other independent stations. Surveys show TV news to be the dominant source of mass information in our society (Roper, 1971), and people believe it to be more credible than other media. The growth and influence of news channels may be the most important—but least understood—of our technological accomplishments. Philip Elliott (1972: 156) notes how the organization behind these channels enables a few people to define what is significant for us all.

> In news bulletins, information about people and events in society comes filtered through the selection and presentation decisions made by television newsmen. Their ideas on what makes news decide which people and issues will receive publicity through the medium.

This is important since we run our lives according to pictures in our heads. As long as many of these images come from TV news, then the work of transforming events into news is an act of power that touches us all. My research leads me to conclude that news messages have played a significant part in our history and will continue to help shape our future. I think that these messages have a far greater impact than the events they are claimed to reflect. This is why all facets of the news process and news perspective must be understood.

● One reason Americans like TV news is that we depend on it. The size and complexity of our cities and country prohibit first-hand experience with many events that influence us. This is especially true in a technological society, where a decision thousands of miles away can affect our personal lives. But technology and size are not the only considerations.

Our society is not an observable thing of a collectivity of shared values and goals. It is a collage of different and often conflicting ethnic and racial groups, religious affiliations, occupational interests, age and sex divisions, and geographical peculiarities. Indeed, it is still an open question whether or not the people living within our borders even constitute a single society. Such diversity does not promote shared experience and understanding. This seething pluralism, plus the vast numbers and daily routines of Americans, makes shared knowledge and interests—the foundation of any social order—difficult to attain. This is why we must understand TV news: It is one of the few things we all have in common.

● Another reason Americans like news is its availability and meaning. The growth of the news business, and especially the advent of television in the last three decades, have led us to expect to know about major events. The coverage of political conventions, state funerals, and spectacular disasters are noteworthy in anyone's book. They are news because they have practical and emotional significance for most people. Though there are few events of this magnitude, the meaning of news is infused with such examples. This is why people tend to equate media presentations with significance; if something is in (on) the news, then it *must* be important. This assumption has been the bread and butter of network TV news for two decades. Local news operations have recently tapped this meaning.

Network and Local News

All TV news is not the same. Just as the practical problems of newspapers distinguish them from TV news, network news operations are distinct from those of "local" stations. We seem to know more about network news than local reports even though local stations put on twice as much news each day.

The history of the expansion of TV networks and the increase in affiliate stations has had a great impact on TV news. The Federal Communications Commission (FCC) limits the number of stations each network may directly control to five. These "owned and operated" stations form but a small part of the network "net," which is made up of independent stations agreeing to "affiliate," or contractually carry network programming for a set fee. This expansion of affiliate stations enables network programs, including news, to reach a larger audience. In their early days, affiliate stations were only channels for network programming. About the only programs that originated locally were wrestling matches and talk shows.

While this comprises the majority of independent stations, there are others which continue to operate autonomously. The expanding market made extended programming more profitable.

Affiliate stations blossomed at quite a pace. Since the 1950s their numbers have more than doubled, until now there are over 600. Most significant is the rapid increase in the amount of daily news presented. Network news reports lasted for about fifteen minutes a day in the early 1950s, and then grew to a half-hour in 1963. There is presently a movement to expand coverage to one hour. The few minutes of local news consisted of reading wire-copy and the newspapers. All this changed by the middle of 1960, when local stations expanded their original programming to include longer news reports. This trend continues into the 1970s. Many stations now have a morning newscast, a noon newscast, and an hour show in the evening, followed by another half-hour report at the end of their daily programming. Some produce two hours or more of locally originated news, and there is talk of even more news programming being added.

These increases are aimed at making money. The formula is quite simple. Expanding local programming provides a forum for presenting more commercials. Local stations get a larger share of this revenue from their own programs than from those which originate at the networks. But the shows they present will make more money if they attract a large audience, which explains why media managers are not always willing to put anything on the air, but prefer to show what they think people will watch. And these days people watch news; thus, news is profitable.

Another reason for expanding news coverage is the onslaught of federal regulations. The Federal Communications Commission (FCC) has been steadily increasing the amount of time that stations must devote to public affairs programming. Their guidelines currently call for fifteen percent of all programming to be devoted to news and public affairs. A few hours of news each week, plus public service announcements, and an occasional talk show about a local issue can cover the requirement. The intent of the FCC was to offset the push for greater profits at the expense of public service. I know of one station which fills an hour of air time each day with news reports and lengthy interviews. The three-man staff is aware that the intent is not to adequately cover the community news, but rather "to keep the FCC off our backs." Fulfilling the FCC guidelines permits the lucrative practice of showing old movies for top advertising dollars. Federal requirements, then, are one reason that news has expanded, but the appeal of other advertising profits should not be overlooked. Despite the fact that network and local operations share this orientation, there are some important differences between them.

Network news differs from local newscasts in several ways. Network staffs are much larger, and correspondents are stationed on various continents and throughout the United States. These correspondents, plus staff members of the five network owned-and-operated stations, provide each major broadcaster with a sizeable crew for special assignments and documentaries. Each employee is a potential source for filling the half-hour of network news, although most of these stories are routinely filed by a handful of correspondents who cover the Washington-New York axis.

Local news operations have fewer employees and a narrower focus. Their news reflects immediate city and metropolitan matters, although several minutes of each of their newscasts will usually be devoted to world and national news. However, the smaller staffs have a greater burden in providing enough material to fill an hour or more of daily newscasts. This amount of coverage produces more profit because the cost of producing an extra half-hour of news is less than the advertising gains for the same period.

Sources of revenue differ in other ways. Network news operations are relatively minor profit makers in the entire television business. While each of the major networks operates in the "black," success is usually evaluated by comparing audience size. If the competition of a single show is doing better in the ratings, the rest of the programming provides more than enough money to make up for loss of advertising revenue; thus, the network is not likely to go bankrupt because of an unpopular news program. By the same token, if the network news does better than its competitors, its profits will greatly increase, because operating costs are relatively fixed but advertisers are billed according to the size of the audience. As one network vice president explained, "It costs the same to reach thirty million as ten million; we just get three times as much money for the same time" if a larger audience tunes in (Epstein, 1973: 83).

Unlike the networks, affiliates spend a disproportionate amount of their budgets on news. At most local stations, news is the single greatest expense. This means that news ratings—the estimates of the size and composition of the viewing audience—have greater significance for local stations than at the networks. Indeed, at many local stations, news either operates in the red or barely breaks even. Another implication is that local stations must be more sensitive to the interests and tastes of their audience. This explains why many local stations retain consultants to find out what the audience wants, what "grabs" them, in order to alter newscasts so that people will watch. This economic pressure also underlies the current "happy talk" format—involving anchormen bantering back and forth in order to entertain viewers—now sweeping America. This strategy often includes clowning with weather reporters and generally having a good time. A sign in Channel B's newsroom captures the gist of this orientation: "Smile, you're going into someone's home with the news." All of this is aimed at doing well in the ratings.

Though networks are economically different from local stations, the former exert pressure on the latter. Most local stations are

affiliated with one of the three major networks, which means that
the networks pay the stations for carrying network programs; the
affiliates actually constitute the "net." Networks rent affiliate
time by paying them thirty percent over what they could earn
from local sponsors to carry the national programs. This source
of income, however, is contingent on maintaining good enough
ratings to give the network its highest share of the audience. If,
for example, one local station is not doing well in the ratings,
another in the same market area could replace it as the network
affiliate. Thus, not only are networks and affiliates different from
an economic standpoint, but the latter depend on the former for
programming and revenue.

The time allotments that must be filled by network and local
stations also influence their respective news sources. Networks
and local stations fill this time in different ways. Networks get
more of their material from the wire services (often as much as
70%), or from stories that are developed by individual producers.
Affiliates, on the other hand, derive half or more of their stories
from press releases and public relations announcements. The remainder of local news items are taken from police or fire department radio monitors. The sources of the news stories are another
important difference between network and local news.

The main news sources for local stations are the dominant institutions and officials. Local station managers are often closer to
city fathers and other influentials than are their network counter-
parts, who have been described as experienced journalists whose
usually liberal politics are relatively unfettered by the leanings of
their superiors. This is not as true at the local level, where affiliate
managers tend to ride with the conservative currents of police
departments, city officials, and businessmen.

One station I studied was run by a man who regularly lunched
and socialized with local officials. His editorials, as well as many
of the news stories he generated, reflected his friends' interests.
Another station was headed by corporate rulers who worried
about controversy and wanted to maintain a "middle-of-the-road"
position. Several other affiliates were supervised by men who
publicly aligned themselves with conservative causes. While not all
managers directly influence the day-to-day news operation, their
political presence is evident.

TV news accommodates the TV business, but it still influences viewers. This is especially true when film enables the audience to see "newsworthy" people, places, and situations. In light of the expansion of this important medium, and the influence it has—both presumed and actual—it is important to understand how newswork contributes to the images we are shown. This entails a brief examination of the conception and sources of bias.

News Bias

Bias refers to distortion which clouds the truth. As types of bias are held in check, the true, or objective, character will shine through. According to this common conception of objectivity, there is believed to be a "world out there" with an inner truth, a view of objectivity which has spawned the common phrase, "We don't make the news; we report it." Richard Salant, the President of CBS News once said, "Our reporters do not cover stories from their point of view. They are presenting them from nobody's point of view." These beliefs lead many contributors to news messages to agree that the stories they tell mirror reality. As CBS anchorman Walter Cronkite often puts it, "That's the way it is." Moreover, this objective nature of things is believed to exist independently of human intentions, interpretations, and meanings, although these may be a source of bias. While it is apparent that, from this perspective, all potential bias may not be recognized, some journalists are aware that merely presenting the "facts" is not enough because they are often "somebody's facts." One experienced reporter explained (Malloy, 1975):

> You've got to make a judgment about what a candidate really means. Say he goes into a goat dance about how 'I'm not gonna be a candidate.' And all the time you know he's got people out and he's building an organization. If you don't report that, you're misleading your readers.

Even though political observers, journalists, and social scientists agree that the facts are not clear-cut, most employ recipes to reduce bias. There are, however, disagreements about what the major sources of bias are. Indeed, the current controversies surrounding journalism in general, and especially TV news, suggest that common interest in objective analysis is divided on the proper method or technique for "getting the facts," on the one hand, and assessing how objective these facts are, on the other.

One source of confusion and conflict over the nature of news in American life—and increasingly throughout the Western world—is the way the problem of objectivity is conceived; this influences how various critics aim to solve it. Illuminating some conceptions of objectivity as it relates to news clarifies its subjective nature and shows how each version leads to a specific solution of the problem. My treatment of these versions of objectivity as "perspectives" will be followed by an alternative formulation which ties news bias to the news process itself.

THE POLITICAL PERSPECTIVE ON NEWS BIAS

The perspective of news evaluators is an important part of their assessment of news practices. Politically oriented critics tend to see news stories as reflecting the viewpoint of the opposition. They believe values to be the primary source of bias: The reporter's personal or political outlook on an issue prevents him from seeing the correctness of the other side. Liberals and conservatives each argue that news is tilted toward the other side; they feel that journalists with false ideas of reality or vested interests overlook what is really significant and true. According to this view, ideological expediency is traded for "objective" analysis, and the viewers are deluded, "brainwashed," "fed propaganda," and, in general, misled. The attacks on the mass media by former Vice President Agnew, and the charges of media critics like Edith Efron (1971) illustrate the conservative stance. Their analyses argue that TV news, and especially the networks, are liberal and anti-Republican.

Liberal counter-claims—especially the more convincing ones—are likely to emphasize how prevailing values, options, and definitions of reality are often explicitly, but usually implicitly, part of news messages. For example, Herbert Marcuse (1964), a philosopher and scholar of Marxist thought, argues that more of our thinking is geared to a kind of economic and calculating logic, which he refers to as one-dimensional. The prevalence of widely accepted values in news reports about "American life" would qualify as examples of distorted communication (Mueller, 1973). While differing in several ways, both sides agree that cutting through values and ideological tendencies would present a truer picture of reality. From this perspective, one solution is to make one's values explicit; another is to employ reporters and commentators of different political persuasions.

THE JOURNALISTIC PERSPECTIVE ON NEWS BIAS

Journalists are sensitive to the charge of political motivation, and most deny that their values color the stories they present. To the contrary, journalists often interpret charges of bias to be an indication of objective reporting—especially when liberals and conservatives make the charges simultaneously. Journalists argue that being attacked by both sides is evidence that their coverage is fair. From this point of view, values can be adjusted for by giving both sides and "telling it down the middle."

However, journalists are aware that ethical issues may also compromise objective reporting. From their perspective, being fair in their coverage and thorough in their research are ways to insure better reporting. For example, some journalists feel that invasion of a newsworthy personality's privacy compromises their craft. A reporter (Malloy, 1975) for a large Chicago paper puts it this way:

> My main ethical consideration always has been not to mess around with the private lives of public people. If an alderman is sleeping with someone on the side, I don't want to know that stuff. It makes me nervous, this stuff you hear nowadays about how reporters are going to have to poke into the private lives of public figures. If we do that, then Nixon would have been justified to go poking into our private lives. . . . You get to screwing with a guy's private life and you wreck his wife, you wreck his kids. We have no right to be so destructive.

Another ethical issue for TV journalists involves staging, or arranging for an event to happen in order to film it. A Chicago television station's coverage of a "pot party" in 1967 is one example. The ethics of the report were questioned since the students arranged with the TV crew the time and place of the "party." The violence-ridden demonstrations at the Democratic Convention in 1968 are another example. One cameraman knew that a sign reading "Welcome to Chicago" had been deliberately set on fire for filming purposes, but the story was shown as though he had just happened upon it. But this aspect of ethics is also ambiguous. A TV producer explained (Malloy, 1975):

> Say you're following a candidate around and he wants to go into a barbershop and shake hands. There's nothing wrong with asking him to wait a minute while you go in there and set up [cameras] first. But if the barbershop is empty, it is wrong to bring people in.

Many journalists feel that adopting a set of rules would help reduce such bias.

While journalists are aware of the importance of values and ethics, they also realize that other considerations—such as commercialism and presentation strategies—influence news coverage. Probably the most famous case of commercialism influencing the news is Fred Friendly's (1967) experience as President of CBS News. He resigned his post when his superiors would not interrupt a fifth rerun of "I Love Lucy" to show Congressional Hearings on U.S. involvement in Vietnam. According to Friendly, economics outweighed the public interest: Lucrative commercials would be lost if Lucy were preempted. Other journalists (cf. Halberstam, 1976), especially those in TV, realize that selling products depends on capturing the largest share of the audience (Malloy, 1975).

> News is saleable, marketable. . . . The size of the audience and the composition of the audience determines how much you can charge for a minute or 30 seconds of [commercial] time. You've got to give the audience what they want, but you don't want to prostitute yourself.

Another journalist agrees (Malloy, 1975):

> I say television news is entering the beer-and-pizza era. Give them what they want, not what's nutritious. What's good for them and what's attractive and tasty are not always the same.

The movement to "give them what they want" has spawned lucrative consulting services which survey the audience and then advise management on the best way to cover and present the news. The aim, of course, is to attract viewers (Malloy, 1975).

On some [local] stations the survey is king. If the surveys say the audience wants crime stories instead of politics, they'll shove in every cheap crime story. If they say the audience loses interest after 20 seconds, all of your stories run 20 seconds.

The name of the TV news game is to capture the greatest share of the audience as reflected in rating points: "One rating point can mean a million dollars' worth of advertising in this town" (Malloy, 1975). And in another city, a member of the sales staff told me,

On any program that when the viewing diminishes to a point where clients do not want to buy advertising in it, and you can't even crack the nut for the cost of the program, then a businessman has to take a hard look at that.

From this perspective, quality of news is evaluated quantitatively, although not all journalists would agree with the commercial criterion as stated by one reporter: "We're beating the competition two to one in the ratings so our news must be good." Some journalists I interviewed feel that the preoccupation with commericalism and "playing to the numbers" distorts news reports. These detractors believe that such bias can be reduced by taking business out of news and letting the professionals do their work.

THE SOCIAL SCIENCE PERSPECTIVE ON NEWS BIAS

Social scientists are also aware of factors which intervene between an event and how it is reported. A number of social science researches of news may be seen as verification of Walter Lippmann's (1922: 222) observation more than fifty years ago that the editor's stereotypes influence what is selected and that

the thing [news] could not be managed at all without systematization, for in a standardized product there is economy of time and effort, as well as a partial guarantee against failure.

For example, the classic study by David Manning White (1950) of "gatekeeping," or the way editors select a few news items from hundreds of potential stories, spawned two decades of similar research on newspapers, radio, and television (Lewin, 1949). Other researchers, like Warren Breed (1955), show the way pressure exacts conformity in a newsroom; reporters learn what management wants and then pursue what is in their own best interests (Tunstall, 1972). Other argue that the organizational requirements imposed on reporters to fill time and space with exclusive but verified reports promotes a reliance on officials who have insider understandings of the political process (Gieber and Johnson, 1961). As journalists fulfill their practical requirements, officials are able to promote their versions of policy and even use the news media to communicate "what is happening" to their superiors, foreign governments, and the public at large. Thus, the emergent reciprocity turns the news channels into a kind of bulletin board that is carefully edited for purposes other than merely "getting all the facts" (cf. Sigal, 1973). It is the news value, rather than explicit political values, which perpetuates this situation. The impact of news values is illustrated by part of a memo authored by renowned journalist David Broder upon his resignation from the New York *Times* (Roshco, 1975: 110).

> In general, it was my impression that Times editors had a certain few stimuli to which they reacted in a political story: Instances of extremism, either of the New Left or the Radical Right; political action by southern (but not northern) Negroes; Kennedy stories of any variety. These may be the grist of political talk at New York cocktail parties, but, as you know, they do not begin to embrace the variety of concerns that really animate national politics.

Social scientists also point to scheduling pressures, the reliance on certain news sources, and other organizational demands as further compromising objectivity. Elliott's (1972) study of a British documentary team showed that messages were selected on the basis of their acceptance by members of the media culture rather than of independent analysis. Epstein (1973) describes the way time and scheduling constraints encourage network news people to use items from four or five cities in presenting "national news." And network coverage of the Vietnam war illustrates how organizational concerns can promote distorted reports. New York producers, rather than field correspondents, selected the major topics for presenting the war in a systematic way and linking one brief report to the next. For example, prior to 1968, the focus was on the American military initiative and the steady stride toward victory. The Tet offensive in 1968 helped change this theme to note the danger American soldiers were in and that the "light at the end of the tunnel" was growing dimmer. The focus shifted again in 1969 to "Vietnamization," and the way the South Vietnamese military was shouldering more of the burden. This was followed by evening news reports of the peace talks in Paris. As one network producer put it after deciding that peace negotiations were the lead story, "Combat stories seemed like a contradiction and would confuse the audience." For Epstein, organized news practices lead to the omission of some stories and approaches in favor of others.

Epstein, Elliott, and the others I cited do not make specific recommendations for changing news, but several changes are implicit in their analyses. The various "gatekeepers" which mold raw events into news stories tend to distort what actually occurs (cf. Molotch and Lester, 1974). This problem can presumably be reduced, if not solved, by making the process more rational and less arbitrary. This orientation leads one social scientist to conclude that current programming for "power and profit" not only "perpetuates the American way," but also "makes a farce of the notion that the United States encourages a free marketplace of ideas" (Tuchman, 1974: 38-39). According to this view, restructuring the economics and control of broadcasting in general, and of news in particular, will go far toward remedying hegemony. This is an important, but incomplete statement of a more pervasive bias.

Each of the critical standpoints agrees that bias distorts the news picture, but their critiques are mild compared to those of Marshall McLuhan (1960, 1962, 1964, 1967) and his followers. For McLuhan, each medium influences the message it transmits. Touch, voice, print, and electronic imagery contribute to perception and interest in messages. From this perspective, the medium is more important than the message: People will be more influenced by the television medium than by message content. It is easy to extend McLuhan's analysis to TV news: The main bias is in the electronics rather than in the work which promotes events as news. Like the other critiques, this is an important but limited understanding of TV news.

THE NEWS PERSPECTIVE AS BIAS

Each of the previous assessments of news overlooks how news decontextualizes an event—removes it from the context in which it occurs. Instead, the critics focus on a world "out there" to be reported, which makes bias anything which distorts the true meaning—the objective nature—of an event.

My focus in this book is on the news perspective as bias. *I argue that the organizational, practical, and other mundane features of newswork promote a way of looking at events which fundamentally distorts them.* As procedures and understandings change, so does news reporting. How news shows are produced and the way news imputes meaning and significance to people and events are the central concerns of this book. Unlike McLuhan's contention that the electronic imagery is the significant feature of television, I suggest that the perspectives and practical procedures which give us the shows, especially the nightly news, are also an influential medium; people's images of reality are not just derived from the TV medium per se, but are consequences of the *way* television is used in presenting news messages.

Daily life is too complex for a reporter's brief examination, and communication between people depends on shared understandings and experience. This means· that everyday life occurs in familiar contexts and can only be understood by those who are familier with its context. Unless a reporter shares these meanings, he/she will not fully grasp an event. But current news practices treat events as though they have objective qualities independent of the motives, purposes, and understandings of the people involved. The world of commonplace occurrence is not approached with uncertainty, but is instead conceived and then molded through news procedures in order for it to be reported on.

This is why I say TV news is a medium in its own right. It has its own context and interest in presenting events-as-news. In the process of presentation, the world of everyday life is transformed for news purposes. The effect is to take an event out of its familiar circumstances and surroundings and meanings, and then embed it in a foreign situation—a news report. Thus, in order to make events news, news reporting decontextualizes and thereby changes them. Thus, news stories will usually be irremediably biased—although the distorting influence of the news process can be illuminated, taken into account, and to that extent reduced.

As I emphasize in the final chapter, TV news does not merely inform us about events in terms of who, what, where, when, and why. Rather, TV news provides a scene for events; it is the medium through which more and more public events are recognized, selected, reported, and presented. Public impact is even greater when we remember that newscasts are the main arena for public recognition of significant issues and events. This is the most crucial aspect of TV news, and one which many analysts have hitherto overlooked. The changing character of news in the past hundred years reflects the emphasis today's newscasts have on the public.

AMPLIFICATION AND IMPACT OF TV NEWS

Modern news organizations, and especially TV news, are changing the individual's role in defining what is newsworthy. News is presented differently than it used to be, and its character has altered. Mass news did not exist until the nineteenth century when the "penny press" spawned commercialism, sensationalism, and rational efforts to communicate with the public (Hughes, 1940). Prior to that time, individuals obtained information they were interested in, and which usually had direct relevance to their lives, safety, or business. For the most part, news consisted of one person giving another some information about crises, situations like natural disasters. Indeed, studies of rumor show that people today often prefer these channels of "improvised news" when conventional news channels are either unable or not available to resolve ambiguous situations (Shibutani, 1966; Klapp, 1972: 213-259). Historically then, news was sought to clarify a personal situation. With few exceptions, viewers seldom watch the evening news *in order to* learn about topics experienced independently of news channels. Rather, people "watch the news" *because* that is where newsworthy events are presented. The institutionalization of news messages has become a sanctioned activity. In the process of watching the news, people learn what is significant from the standpoint of those who work within practical and organizational limitations to find, schedule, film, and report events-as-news. Thus, most significant events are learned about as news stories whether or not they ever become personally relevant.

An event may become interesting and socially significant after a lot of people know about it. The event thereby becomes more important, and in some instances, its influence may be fundamentally changed. This *amplification* process is a consequence of the organization and meaning of news, and it is clearly evident in the news coverage of Senator Thomas Eagleton's history of mental health in 1972, which I will discuss in Chapter 6. In an editorial calling for Eagleton's resignation as the Democratic vice-presidential candidate, the Washington *Post* concluded: "It is our judgment that the burden imposed by the presence of Senator Eagleton on the ticket can only be removed by his withdrawal as a candidate."

One researcher (Young, 1973: 352) found the press interest in combatting the use of marijuana in Britain to have an effect on police tactics:

> The moral panic over drug use was initiated in [Britain] by the police approaching journalists and informing them that 'the situation had got out of hand.' The mass media responded enthusiastically and police of all ranks become exposed to a playback and subsequent elaboration of their prejudices.

Some research shows the media to have little impact (cf. Hubbard et al., 1975), but other studies show a relationship between what people see on the nightly news and what they regard as problems and issues (Cohen and Young, 1973). Research has found that voters believe that the important issues in an election are those that receive most coverage on television (McCombs and Shaw, 1972). The same is true with mental illness (Nunally, 1961), and attitudes toward the Vietnam war (Epstein, 1973). Many individual ideas about important and meaningful events are publicly generated by news organizations. This is most clearly seen by reflecting on the dominant issues of the last decade: race relations, poverty, war, ecology, and political corruption. All have been presented as news stories. But the most striking thing about them is that they were serially presented even though they existed simultaneously and can still be found. The public was aroused about these issues, but only after each had been treated as news.

These examples suggest that news messages may do more than inform viewers about events; they may also change the meaning and significance of events. Just as speech infuses and shapes social situations, TV news coverage molds public events. Just as some people become skilled in language use to seduce others, sell products, get votes, and bring the "wayward" to salvation, public relations spokespersons, press secretaries, and police chiefs promote their causes through news reports. Daniel Boorstin (1961) has shown that media coverage promotes "pseudo events," or happenings that are staged for the media. Press conferences—practically always self-serving—are the best example.

But events also change *for* the media. This has greater impact on everyday life than Boorstin's pseudo events which are actually created for the media. Most social situations are not created for publicity purposes—and only a few would not exist if the mass media disappeared. But many are altered for public consumption. The National Political Conventions are one example, which I will discuss in Chapter 5. Another type takes in a lot of territory: official reports and information provided to the mass media by various individuals, groups, and organizations, such as politicians, police officers, and truck drivers, who know that their media images will be the public image. Law makers, law breakers, social movements, and social prophets are media-wise, and they use this wisdom to attract the public eye and to influence policy. (I present examples of these media strategies in Chapter 4.)

It is a mistake to see TV as merely reporting events and not influencing them. But it is also incorrect to see the TV camera only as a forum for an individual or group to do something which would not otherwise occur. My research shows that TV coverage alters many social situations by changing everyday life. Thus, TV watchers must learn how to watch the news, and TV personnel must become aware of the process which not only transforms events into news, but is changing public conceptions of issues and problems. Thus, while TV news may give us a *superficial acquaintance with* some events, these reports are helping to shape the public consciousness and, therefore, the future of our society.

An informed citizenry must have more *detailed knowledge about* the news process. It is essential that we learn to watch the news defensively, in order to know which questions to ask and how to be critical. Once viewers acquire this competence, distinctions can be drawn between sound and distorted reports. Hopefully, news procedures will change to resolve the problems I focus on. If this does not occur—and in all likelihood it will not immediately happen—then more responsibility is heaped on the viewer to demystify the news perspective in specific instances. This requires the recognition and understanding that news is a product of practical tasks designed to resolve organizational problems. Clarifying the way news gets done, its objectivity, adequacy, and social usefulness, cannot be accomplished without considering what these practicalities contribute to the news.

Chapter 2

THE NEWS ENVIRONMENT

There are three overriding and interdependent contributors to the news scene: commercialism and ratings; competition with other stations; and the community context, especially political ties.

Commercialism

Commercialism did not begin with television. Robert E. Park (1923: 80) has shown that the "Natural History of the Newspaper" is "the history of this surviving species. It is an account of the conditions under which the existing newspaper has grown up and taken form." This process included changing from "party" newspapers, or explicitly partisan "newssheets," to independent newspapers which were supported by broader circulation. The long-term effect on modern journalism has been well stated by DeFleur (1970: 14):

> The foundation of an important institutionalized pattern of social relationships which linked advertiser, media operators, and audience into a functional system for the production of particular types of mass communicated content, were worked out in the early years of the development of the mass press.

The first success was Benjamin Day's New York *Sun* in 1833. This so-called "penny paper" was contingent on "advertisements and cash purchases as the only source of revenue" (Hughes, 1940: 7). The years that followed saw other papers enter the "independent" market and the beginnings of the reciprocal interchange between "news" and "advertising."

> What the advertiser bought was circulation, and his money paid the costs of publishing the paper. Sales of the newspapers to readers barely paid for the ink and newsprint paper. But to make advertising space worth paying for, there must be wide circulation. The circulation liar was an inevitable phenomenon in a period when, to survive, it was necessary to boast. Circulation was achieved through the news columns [Hughes, 1940: 16].

Concern with profits grew concomitantly with news interest. The crowning point of this era of zealous commercialism was the emergence of the "yellow press." The changed emphasis on circulation is still felt in all forms of journalism.

> The fundamental change in journalism brought about by the Yellow Press was the complete concentration on the production of a commodity or something that would sell. The missionary conception of his profession that had fortified the political editor had given way to the business attitude [Hughes, 1940: 22].

In Will Irwin's (1911: 18) words,

> We will give the public what it wants, without bothering to elevate the commonwealth. If we find that people prefer murders, then murders they shall have.

The total impact was clear (Hughes, 1940: 23):

> Every change in the newspaper, since, has been to perfect it as a commodity—that is, to make it responsive to its market. Sixty years before, "upstairs" (i.e., editorial staff) had wholly dominated the newspaper, but the balance of power had now shifted in the direction of "downstairs" (i.e., business staff).

Like newspapers, television programming is aimed at profits.

While the former sells space to advertisers, the latter sells "air time." But how much the time will cost depends on the number, and demographic characteristics, of the viewers. The "ratings" provide station managers with this "objective" information, and in the process guarantee that all TV programming will be a marketplace first, and a forum for ideas and issues second.

THE RATINGS

TV news, like all other programming, makes money by selling a certain chunk of the audience to an advertiser for a specified time, such as thirty seconds or one minute. The programs are intended to attract the viewers to the commercial messages. But the viewers cannot be sold if they cannot be counted. This is what the ratings do.

Economic interest in the size and (demographic) shape of the audience (read "market") required an accounting procedure acceptable to the buyer and the seller. The stations needed an audience gauge to translate viewers into dollars per minute. Likewise, the buyers wanted assurance that their messages were being received by the relevant "demographics"—e.g., women aged 18-49. The answer was found in probability theory, and especially the "central-limit theorem" and the "law of large numbers." These principles underlie statistical inference whereby a random sample of viewers can be said to represent the population. Rating services contributed to the commercialization of television by providing the means to numerically estimate the nature of the market. According to the A. C. Nielsen Company (1964: 3), one of the largest rating services, "In television, an audience rating is a statistical estimate of the number of homes viewing a program as a percent of all homes having a television set." The relationship among the sellers (TV stations), the buyers (advertisers), and the rating services can be simply stated: (1) Television staffs sell access to the audience; (2) advertisers buy this air time; (3) the rating services provide the "official" market.

On the basis of this statement, programming decisions could now be "scientifically" assessed. If low ratings reduced the selling price, and if this was the most relevant consideration, then those programs which "captured" the largest share of the audience for would-be sponsors were likely to be pursued by the programming department. This link of seller, buyer, and market is the basic reason for cancelling programs, for having few in-depth documentary reports, and, in general, for using television for entertainment.

The A. C. Nielsen Company and the American Research Bureau (ARB) "measure" viewing habits throughout the country, but their methods vary depending on whether they are measuring network programming or "local" markets. If the former, approximately 1,100 "representative" homes (e.g., according to age, sex, family size, ethnicity, and region) are contacted. Those agreeing to participate in the survey have audimeters installed in their homes. This device records whether the TV receiver is "on," and, if so, which channel is tuned in. At a designated time, the tapes are mailed to the Nielsen Company, where the audience responses are converted to data cards and then extrapolated to the entire population. Numerical accounts are then provided on: percentage of families viewing each broadcast at fifteen-minute intervals; each program's share of the audience watching anything at a particular time; and the number and percentage of viewers according to age and sex. The latter information is especially useful for the television sales staff in "hitting" certain "targets." A member of Channel B's sales staff explained:

> If we're selling women's girdles, we probably should not be playing in the middle of baseball. If we're selling a soap product or a toothpaste we probably should be hitting in the center of a family or a woman's program, because the most important demographic, and that is a word we use to talk about the audience composition, is women 18 to 49. Why? Because women 18 to 49 control the pursestrings of the average family.

The mechanics of the sampling, extrapolation, and use of audimeters have been harshly criticized by Harry Skornia (1965: 129). After noting that only about fifty-seven percent of those randomly selected will permit audimeters to be installed in their homes, he adds,

> At any given time probably not more than about nine hundred of the Nielsen Audimeters across the country are in working order. Of those turned on, depending on the competition which in turn determines

how many ways the audience is split, in a typical area, perhaps 32 sets may be tuned to one station, 24 to another, and so on. Since about 25 percent of the films are not usable because of human or mechanical failure, these 32 or 24 are reduced to 24 and 18 respectively. These sets bear the burden of reflecting the nation's taste. The House Committee which investigated ratings in March, 1963 found that one of the sets had been on over twenty-four hours. One Nielsen customer explained that she had turned the set on as a baby sitter. Another noted that the Nielsen-equipped set was in the children's bedroom, where no one else watched. In some cases, there may be only two or three Audimeters in a given city. Such is the so-called rating research carried out with Audimeters and similar attachments. By concealing the small numbers involved in the sample through the simple device of transforming them into percentages, the illusion of adequacy is created.

Audimeters are not used in "local" market surveys.

Western City, where I conducted much of my research, is rated four times a year by the Nielsen Company and three times annually by ARB. Rating periods last for approximately one month. There are estimated to be 451,000 and 456,000 TV households in Western City by Nielsen and ARB, respectively. From this population, a residential telephone directory aides in the selection of a "representative" sample of 1,000. Of the original 1,000, between 560 and 600 households agree to fill out viewing "diaries." The sample size is then split into four sections, one section for each of the four weeks of the "rating period"—e.g., October 26-November 22. Upon completion of the "rating period," the diaries are collected, the data analyzed, and an "average viewing week" is presented as "ratings" in Nielsen's *Viewers in Profile* and the *ARB Audience Estimates.*

Despite the appeal of these "scientific" numbers, not all parties in the news scene agree on their meaning or significance. Examining and evaluating how the various contributors to the rating information understand their tasks is a preview of the different—and often conflicting—approaches to the news. Important differences between those who assign stories and those who actually report about events will be more fully discussed in the next chapter. For now, the different perspectives on the ratings can be used to illustrate the different interests in the news within the TV station. The remainder of this section shows how the rating process is transformed into "official statistics" to be used by media managers to make decisions about TV news.

Beginning with the audience who fill out the "rating diaries," the numbers are launched on what might be termed an organizational career. When and if the representative sample returns the viewing diaries to the rating service, the results are categorized with predefined codes. The report is then passed to subscribing advertisers as well as to the sales staff of the TV stations which uses these numbers to promote commercial messages. The third party to use these numbers to reflect his perspective on news is the station manager who makes changes and offers suggestions in the hope of raising a particular program's ratings. Finally, the newsworkers join the effort to treat these indicators of the news operation's strengths and weaknesses, and essentially verify what they already believe to be true.

Stage 1: Respondents and the Ratings. It is commonplace that any data are only as good as their source. This takes on more significance with television ratings since those who provide the primary data seem less interested in doing a good job of filling out the viewing diary as directed, than they are with "getting it done" because "it's such a pain in the ass." At any rate, the meaning of this diary account to those who do it provides a basis for comparing other uses of these "data."

Several important assumptions underlie diaries as a data source. Foremost is the idea that the rating diaries are filled out while people watch the program—i.e., every fifteen minutes a notation will be made. In other words, the viewer's response is believed to more or less correspond with what he or she actually watched, especially since it is assumed that very little time separated the "watching" from the "noting." Of course, subscribers to the rating services are told in "fine print" about possible problems.

Simple basic instructions in the diary aid accurate and complete entries of stations, channels and programs viewed for more than five minutes and the individuals viewing. Subscribers are reminded that diary-keeping is necessarily entrusted to the cooperating households and may thus in part reflect estimates or hearsay. *In other words, the recorded diary data—both viewing and demographic information—are subject to response error* [Nielsen Station Index, 1971; italics added].

ARB also cautions its clients,

> The diary contains specific instructions to record viewing and tuning. The data are affected to the extent that these instructions are understood and followed by the diary keepers.
>
> Some diary entries may have been made on the basis of hearsay, recall, or the estimates of the diary keeper.
>
> It is possible that human and computer processing errors may occur after the diaries are received at ARB headquarters. Consequently, *the degree of variance in the data may be greater than that expected from the sampling variation alone* [italics added].

We do not know how great the "degree of variance in the data" is, and the television industry has done little to find out. Even though programming decisions which influence what millions of viewers see are made on the basis of these data, one searches in vain for a systematic study of the rating process (cf. Evans, 1969; Bechtel et al., 1972). The networks and the Television Information Office have done little to investigate the rating process. I suggest that one reason may be that the results would be irrelevant to current programming practices; even if the studies revealed that the ratings were not reflecting what evaluators think they should, the practical problem of having something to account for commercial charges would remain. My research did not focus on the rating process in detail, except to note how various contributors to the news brew interpret and use these official numbers. I was able to audio-record one couple filling out an ARB rating diary. These comments are provided to illustrate something of the diary process and not as a definitive statement about all rating information, although interviews with a dozen other "rating participants" in two states corroborate these materials. But this case study does provide significantly more information than is currently available about the meaning of viewing diaries in particular, and the rating process in general.

My viewers relied on *TV Guide* to remind them what they had watched the previous week despite the diary instructions to record their selections every fifteen minutes.

P.: What about the *TV Guide;* are you going to use that?

K.: No, I know what I watch, I told you that.

P.: How do you know what I watch?

K.: You can fill out what you watch (laughs).

P.: They should have their things set up from Sunday to Sunday or whatever the *TV Guide* does because that would make it a lot easier.

The "diary" instructions imply that people are aware of very basic information such as how many channels they receive.

K.: Okay, what channels do we get: 2, no; 3, no; 4, no.

P.: We get 4.

K.: Four, we don't get, we don't watch anything on 4.

P.: We do if there is something good on that isn't on 8 or 10, I mean. We can get 4 well enough to watch it but not very often. . . . We get 9 . . . we get 11 . . . we get 13 . . . okay, we get Channel 15.

K.: We don't get that well enough to watch anything.

P.: Yes we do. Sure we do.

K.: We do not.

P.: We do too. We do. All you have to do is hook up the regular antenna to the UHF antenna and it works. I found this out the other night . . . we get 39, too.

Another assumption the rating people make is that people are aware of what they watched.

K.: Did we watch *Adam-12* on Wednesday night?

P.: Is *Adam-12* on Wednesday night?

K.: We just got through watching it tonight [Wednesday] . I hope it is.

P.: Okay, now wait a minute now. *Adam-12* isn't on.

K.: On Wednesday.

P.: No, not at 7:00.

K.: At 7:30.

P.: We watched the *Untamed World.*

K.: I assume that you watched the news yesterday?

P.: Oh yeah.

K.: We're very predictable, dear. That's what this really shows.

P.: No, it doesn't really, because I haven't watched the news every day.

K.: Yes, you do.

P.: No, I don't.

K.: Yes, you do, too.

P.: No, I don't.

K.: Oh no, no, we watched *You Asked For It.*

P.: But that isn't on.

K.: But that's what we watched.

P.: It isn't on tonight.

K.: Uh, huh.

P.: This is December 20 right? At 7:00, it *(TV Guide)* has *Truth or Conse-quences* . . . we're in trouble, dear.

K.: We watched *You Asked For It.*

P.: That was on at 7:30. At 7:00, we eat dinner and we don't really watch anything although we do have the *Untamed World* on this set out here [i.e., in the kitchen]. Now are you going to move to this other book here and say that we watch *Untamed World?*

K.: I am not!

P.: Dear, come on, it's important . . . actually we have both of them [i.e., sets] going at the same time usually because you're in here doing this [i.e., cooking] and I'm out there watching the news.

K.: Well this is absurd (laughter)!

Since this part of the "representative" sample had two televisions, they were given two diaries to fill out, but there was a problem because one set had been loaned to a friend halfway through the week.

P.: No, now wait though; you had to use this set only [i.e., the big TV] be-cause this set we had given to Pat.

K.: I see, what do you suppose he was watching (laughs)?

P.: Do you suppose we ought to give him the pad to fill out between Wed-nesday and Sunday (laughs)?

The issue is resolved.

P.: What are we going to do with this one [i.e., the other diary]? Are you going to keep this one? Maybe we ought to write on this one that the set broke or something like that, do you think, and return it empty because . . . they have got to have it back.

K.: Tell them that was the week we loaned the second TV to friends; that's reasonably true; true is true.

P.: But it isn't entirely true.

K.: Well, the damn thing hasn't been on like 5 minutes in the last month.

P.: Well, okay.

The problems with accounting for time spent watching television are added to when regular programming is interrupted. This occurred when a space shot delayed programming.

P.: Channel 24 is the *Mystery Movie,* but they interrupted that with the splashdown, or the take off.

K.: Well, I don't care what they did . . . we didn't change the channels.

P.: Actually it went on for 45 minutes or so beyond 10:00; we don't know when it was? What are we going to do, lie?

K.: It was a half-hour.

P.: Okay, then we're a half-hour off. Wasn't that the night that we had to call down and find out what the hell happened because everything was off? That happened several times recently. So *Cannon* was at 10:00.

D.A.: You watched *Cannon* at 10:00? Did it come on at 10:00?

P.: No, probably not.

K.: (laughs) This must be the week before.

P.: I wonder if they check that, that would be real interesting.

K.: Well, if they would, it just blew their whole study.

Finally, the general feeling about doing this kind of accounting was obvious.

D.A.: That goddamn thing is complicated.

P.: That's why K. is doing it. [He then discusses her banking experience.]
That took almost an hour and 15 minutes to do. One of the main
problems with this is that when you watch television this is the
worst thing to do because it takes a certain amount of time and
ability to concentrate on . . . something about it ought to be simpli-
fied . . . it interrupted my TV watching (laughs).

Once the diaries are filled out, mailed in, and analyzed, the information is converted to "rating points." In the Western City
market, each "rating point," or the number of homes viewing a
program as a percentage of all homes having a television set, represents roughly 4,500 homes. These summaries are presented in the
Nielsen and ARB booklets somewhat as follows:

MONDAY-FRIDAY: 5:30 p.m. (Newstime)

CHANNEL	RATING	SHARE
D	5	9
A	17	34
B	10	21
E	2	3
F	7	14

A brief interpretation may be helpful. This table presents the rating information on each of the five Western City stations. Rating
services compute two measures of viewer choices—the "rating"
and the "share." Each refers to the percentage of viewers tuned
to a station at a certain time, but there is an important difference.
"Rating" refers to the percentage of *all sets in the market area*
that are tuned to a channel. Thus ten percent of all sets in the
Western City area were tuned to Channel B at 5:30 p.m. "Share"
is computed to determine *how many sets that are tuned on are
tuned in to a given channel*. Referring back to the table shows that
Channel B had a twenty-one percent "share" of the audience
members who were watching anything. The "share" is the more
important number because that indicates how well a station is
doing compared to its competition. Stated differently, it is more
important to show that viewers who watch the news watch your
show, than to suggest that some people just don't watch TV at
this particular hour. The former viewers may be persuaded to try

Channel B, but the latter must first be convinced to turn their TV receivers on!

Once all the data are in, the business of television can proceed. This is where the second stage makes its own contribution to the ratings.

Stage 2: Sales and the Ratings. Just as the viewers have their interpretation of the ratings, so does the sales division at Channel B. They are less interested in how the data are arrived at than in how they are to be used. I talked with a salesman about this.

D.A.: Do you have any idea how big this sample is?

Sales: Yes, I think it's about 1500. I'm not exactly sure but I presume that they try to get that split apart into certain kinds of educational groups and things like that . . . income groups, etc. But that's something that ARB takes care of. *It's hard enough to take one of these books apart without worrying about how they do it.* We pay them a lot of money to do it by the way [italics added].

The overall use of the ratings can now be easily understood. A member of the sales staff explained.

But, at any rate the basic reason that Sales uses this is that we have to have some justification for setting prices, and we have to have some idea what the target audience is. For example, if a car dealer comes on the air, he probably shouldn't be playing in this morning's cartoons where we're hitting kids between 3 years old and 11 years old.

The practical use of these largely ad hoc diary accounts presented as "objective facts" is complex but fairly specific.

Sales: The stations bear the brunt of [the expense of the rating services], not the advertising agencies who also get these books and use it as a club over our head. Even we are the ones who buy it. The agencies buy out the greatest audience for the dollar spent. And the way that we do, the way we frequently sell on TV and radio is [by] cost per thousand. How many thousand people am I reaching in my target audience [e.g., women 18-49] for the amount of dollar being expended? That's easily done by dividing the number of people in the target into the cost of the spot. Now, we see here that 30 seconds cost $28 in the _____ Show and we are reaching a target audience of 12,000 women which roughly (equals) a little over $2 to reach a thousand people.

D.A.: Can you show me roughly how that $28 is arrived at?

Sales: Yes. The station comes to an arbitrary figure of what they feel they can sell . . . either a rating point or a thousand homes at somewhere in the daytime around $10, maybe in prime time at night, $12 to $14 a rating point. So, if we get a rating of three and our cost in the daytime was roughly $10, that would be 3 x 10; we've got $30; actually about $28.

According to this accounting principle, the higher the ratings, the more money comes into the station. These numbers were important to the news operation since the competition outrated Channel B for two years by a margin of nearly 2 : 1. The newsroom's explanation will be dealt with later in the chapter, but it will be more meaningful when compared to the Sales perspective, especially since the latter exerts tremendous pressure on the former "to do something."

D.A.: How do you alter what you charge compared to another station? That is, if another station is higher [i.e., in the "ratings"] does that affect what you charge for advertising time?

Sales: You mean when it's diametrically opposed to us? Well, let's take our news.

D.A.: Yes, take the news, Channels B and A.

Sales: Okay. Our news has been floundering in the rating area for some time. About two years.

D.A.: What do you consider a good rating?

Sales: Well, it used to be 15. Channel A's rating is between 15 and 18, in other words their news audience is almost double what our news audience is. Interestingly enough, demographically, for the most desired portion of that audience, 18 to 49 women and men, we have more than they do. They have something like 16,000; we have 18,000, 18 to 49, with about half the audience. And, we charge $85 for our news—30 second [commercials], and they charge like $140.

D.A.: May I ask, is there a certain bottom where, let's say, the news could get to, that it simply no longer would pay?

Sales: I would imagine that on any program that when the viewing dimin-
        ishes to a point where clients do not want to buy advertising in it,
        and you can't even crack the nut for the cost of the program, that
        a businessman has to take a hard look at that [italics added].

The "hard look" comes from Management.

Stage 3: Management and the Ratings. It was apparent that
the first two stages in the ratings' career were not the same. The
respondents' interests clearly differed from those of the Sales
division. Still another perspective is that of Management, who
must decide what to do about low ratings.

Apart from relatively straightforward accounting practices, ratings also define "good" and "bad" programming, and by implication, "good" and "bad" work. It was noted above that in order to
earn as much money as possible from advertising, the ratings must
reflect a larger share of the audience than the competition. Programming that brings in the "numbers" is "good" and that which
is less successful is "bad." The primarily descriptive nature of the
ratings to provide an indication of *how many* people are watching
is merged with an interpretive function. Station management not
only looks to the ratings for quantitative assessments of how many
people watch various programs, but they also use these numbers as
explanations of viewing behavior. According to this perspective,
low ratings mean that viewers *choose* to not watch a particular
program. Motives and rationale are attributed to the audience
which are unwarranted by the diary data and warned against by
the rating services. A Nielsen brochure (1964: 12) cautions that
"it makes no sense to talk about the TV tunings of any one sample
home as though it specifically represents other homes presumed to
be similar." Nevertheless, that is exactly what is done!

The Management's efforts to improve the ratings "at all costs"
further indicate the great indecisiveness about "what's wrong."
Attempts to raise Channel B's "floundering news" included presenting the news a half-hour earlier than Channel A's newscast,
format changes such as more "happy talk" between anchormen;
changing sets; framing the anchormen "tighter" in order to bring
them closer to the viewers; and personnel changes—firing the news
director and changing anchormen. All these changes had exasper-
atingly little effect on the ratings.

One reason such efforts were largely unsuccessful was their in-congruity with the original data source. Recall that the interpre-tation and use of the ratings reflect peculiar *interests*. Viewers who provide these data seem to be less concerned about providing objective indications of their feelings, motives, and preferences than about "getting it done." However, both Sales and Manage-ment were shown to act as if this were not the case; they treated this official information as having some correspondence with viewer preferences and the reasoning underlying such choices. The upshot is that each of the three parties discussed thus far brought their own interests to the data, and these were in turn informed by their own meanings. For example, "we have to have some justification for setting prices." In understanding how these parties use the ratings, we have learned something about what is significant for them. Similarly, it will be evident that newsmen's use of this information reflects something about their perspective.

Stage 4: Newsmen and the Ratings. Newsworkers draw on their experience and practical understanding to make sense of ratings. Channel B's staff was vaguely aware that these numbers affected advertising revenue, but they were more conscious of the impact of low ratings on their budget, pressure from the front office, and the news director's moodiness. Burns (1969: 71) has described the anxiety "bad numbers" can generate in another research setting.

> The shock of a reported Audience Response figure of 63 for a pro-gramme in a series which had touched 75 was enough to disrupt the first hour or two of rehearsal of subsequent production. Very little work was done. The atmosphere of dejection deepened with every new arrival. Clusters formed around the leading actors, the floor manager, and the assistant floor manager, with the producer circulating between them and the telephone. The whole assembly was, in fact, engaged in a more preoccupying task than rehearsal for the next show: the search for an explanation.

As one of Channel B's "on-set" directors explained:

Director: The big problem we have now in news is ratings and that's taking everything. The point is we have to bring up our ratings and how we're going to do it, we don't know yet. . . . If we had good ratings now the newsroom could call the shots in the station. And by good

I mean if we beat Channel A by 3 or 4 points (or 5) across the board; not by the 5 or 10 points where they beat us across the board. So ratings continue to be the primary concern of (news director) and literally everybody in the newsroom. . . . News is our biggest money . . . loser . . . now.

Newsworkers, like the Sales staff and station Management, offered their own interpretations of what these figures meant. Understanding why certain accounts and not others are offered further articulates their perspective.

There were several explanations offered for losing the rating race. The same director attributed it to the inconsistent production and organization.

Director: I'd like to talk . . . about my feelings about the whole news show from a technical view-point and the way it's presented on the air. . . . It seems to go in cycles. That is, the production of the news show and the final look of it on the air, which has always been my concern, seems to go in cycles . . . of two or three months. . . . The show could not be smoother if I would dream it so for a couple of months and slowly things start falling apart. B-rolls [i.e., silent film] on news stories suddenly become shorter than they were, and they don't cover the A-rolls [i.e., sound film] completely. . . . Or film commercials will—as we had one tonight—suddenly we'll lose the sound loop. . . . The commands that I give to the floor man are not understood. . . . Things seem to go in cycles and it affects the whole station. . . . A manic-depressive effect almost. It's almost as though the place is going theough a menstrual period . . . I can almost feel them coming on.

The organization of presenting the news was not the only reason given for low ratings. Another suggestion was the anchormen's presentation, and especially the importance of "loosening up."

Director: The highest rated stations are the ones that are putting a lot of nonsense on their show . . . a horse-play format. . . . Channel A had a more folksie attitude all the way through their news presentation. . . . We're very hard-bitten . . . we present a very excellent presentation but like a robot.

[We] have not taken cognizance of the fact that . . . the important thing on the air is the presentation of the news by the newsman. Although I think we have a pretty good news staff now, we're still not enough show biz . . . still not show bizzy enough and people at home, I think, expect to be entertained, especially on a news show.

On another occasion we talked specifically about the anchormen.

Director: [We] talked about the seemingly impossible thing of trying to make the guys loosen up even more on the set and really interrelate to each other and interact with the audience. And that we've been working on for a long time, but we still never get down to it, so . . . uh, although they are loosening up a bit, it may take years for [anchorman] to feel comfortable. Uh, that of course, depends on how they feel on the set that night, if they really feel like goofing off, or. . . .

D.A.: Do you ever talk to those guys, I mean do you ever get together with them and talk to them and you know, and find out how they feel about those things?

Director: Oh sure, I usually say, why don't you loosen up. In fact, tonight I was hitting the key on the P. A., the P. A. system into the studio and telling them things to do because we were really short, trying to happy them up a bit. But, it didn't work out that way . . . and they didn't banter back and forth which is what I had hoped they'd do because we were really short.

Newsmen did not understand the research procedures which provided the numbers, but they did take advantage of the widespread belief in such scientific surveys. Virtually any complaint about the "way things are done around here" has been used to explain poor ratings. For example, one anchorman complained about the news format and argued that the ratings reflect the viewer's rejection of the status quo. On another occasion, he explained that the sportscaster "really wasn't well-liked in Western City and that the ratings showed it." One reporter claimed that there was no direction in the newsroom, "no rudder," and pointed to the latest ARB results for verification. Another added that morale was at an all-time ebb because of the "shit that goes on," and held up the Nielsen rating book as support. Similarly, a past member of the news department felt that Channel A did a better reporting job than Channel B. He said the former had far more content, and that the latter was biased, adding, "their ratings show it." From the members' perspective, the ratings are "proof" that a wide range of problems exist which in turn produce low ratings. If the ratings are high, you are doing things right. Indeed, the staff at Channel A occasionally seemed befuddled over their lead, but nevertheless remained convinced that they were doing the better job: "We're beating the competition two to one in the ratings, so our news must be good."

These figures became accepted as reliable indications of competent newswork, but there were exceptions. These arose when newsmen's common sense told them that the numbers couldn't be high because of quality newswork. The weekend anchormen's standard reply to colleagues' criticisms of his leadership was, "We've got the numbers." I asked one camerman if his show was that good. He explained that the main reason for the numbers wasn't the anchorman; "It couldn't be," but that more people watched on the weekends in order to get the sports scores. On another occasion, a reporter was amazed upon learning that a "nothing news operation" (in another city) "had the numbers." From the newsmen's perspective, then, ratings generally confirm impressions about "the way things are here." Like the three prior stages of the ratings' career, newsmen have their own uses and meanings for these official numbers. The ratings were the "official" source of audience response or feedback, but other forms were eagerly sought, especially since the competition was winning the "numbers" race. There were other ways of obtaining feedback: letters, telephone calls, and comments from friends.

Letters and telephone calls provided personal evidence about specific newswork. The relatively small number of calls and letters were given unwarranted importance, because, like the small sample size of the rating services, a few were taken to indicate the feelings of many (cf. Tuchman, 1969: 5). This "iceberg" assumption is seldom questioned but is regarded as another way to feel the public pulse. Comments ranged from the anchorman's dress, color of ties, and not wearing glasses, to charges of bias.

Callers and letter writers were often interested in the same things, but the latter were taken more seriously. Newsmen would often take time to talk with callers and explain things. For example, one caller accused Channel B of always presenting the Democratic views. In other instances, callers were treated courteously but dismissed as "nuts." One caller gave a reporter a reference in *Intellectual Digest* which provided a different slant on a story. The message was written down but subsequently discarded. This was done in many cases where newsmen did not want to be bothered with the details of a particular call or were simply in a hurry. On the other hand, letters were recordable—that is, they could be filed, passed around the newsroom, and presented to colleagues and management as proof of good work, popularity, and the like. Consequently, newsworkers would encourage some callers to write letters in order to make it more official. This was not always done, but if the caller's comment was regarded as reasonable and useful (read "agreeable") from the newsman's perspective, he would often be encouraged to write to the station. In one instance a caller complained about the news director's handling of the Friday evening *Discussion Show* and wanted him taken off the air. According to the newsman who took the call, the viewer wanted to know if a "petition" with several hundred names would be taken seriously by the station management. The caller was assured that any "petition" would be hand-delivered by this newsman to the proper people. (The extra effort would have been gladly extended, since this newsman passionately disliked the news director.) In short, information more compatible with the receiver's interest was more likely to be disseminated, although selective handling of feedback worked both ways.

Management could also control what newsmen heard from viewers. I asked two fellow graduate students to write letters congratulating Channel B for having both a black and a white anchorman on the morning newscast. According to these people, the messages were never received, although they suspected that negative feedback was having little difficulty getting through. The advantage of letter-writing thus had concomitant disadvantages: Anything tangible could be filed in one's personal records or others might intercept the messages and file them in the wastebasket.

The concern with feedback favored letters over calls, but recorded calls were also given great consideration. Since most feedback came from calls, an accounting scheme was established to record these messages. Most calls taken at the front desk were recorded, but those which made their way through to the newsroom were not. The station kept a close watch on the subject and number of calls on a daily "call sheet." The frequency varied, but the average was around forty per day. Most calls requested information about program times and sports scores. Some calls referred to the news operation: "I want to thank Channel B for the weekend news announcer instead of the regular mushed-mouth man. He's such a delight." The range of topics seemed too great to warrant serious consideration, but this was not the case; the station management paid close attention to this account of viewer interests. Suggestions for change would be made on the basis of a few calls. In fact, several members complained vigorously about the "news operation being run by the call sheet." One man noted that a handful of calls are treated like the world of God and this was unwarranted since "most were kooks anyway." This view seems corroborated from a newsman's perspective when exceptionally well-done stories elicit no viewer response. This apparent inconsistency on the part of viewers frustrates news personnel even more when their own suggestions go unheeded, yet a half-dozen calls cause serious discussion about change. For these reasons, newsworkers often reacted angrily to callers. When a woman complained that a story on a POW's sister who had switched her support from Nixon to McGovern was unfair, the anchorman said, "I think I'll use that tonight." In this way, he sought to strike back at the uninformed viewer who didn't understand the nature of newswork.

The problem of feedback does not end with letters and telephone calls. Another important source of feedback is equally weighted (cf. McQuail, 1969: 92). The station manager's "cronies" are more important for newsroom policies than a reporter's, although the staff is sensitive to any comments made by acquaintances and often translates these into images of the viewer. Two or three opinions about a particular story at a dinner engagement were enough to elevate spirits and convinced newsmen that their work was good. Comments from "real people" are rare for newsworkers, although they do share an abstract idea of who the audience is, and what it wants to see.

THE AUDIENCE

The types of feedback newsworkers receive influences their work in several ways. One the one hand, it is encouraging to get a pat on the back from someone who liked an effort you had a part in. On the other hand, much of the feedback indicates that the viewers do not really understand what news is all about and what news personnel are up against. The general result is for news agents not to think very highly of their viewing audience and to regard them as stupid. This is especially true if the ratings are lower than those of a competing station. The Sales and Management people often blame poor ratings on the poor quality of the news staff. This means that low ratings communicate to newsworkers that the viewers are rejecting their efforts, and may even be jeopardizing their jobs if management decides to clean house in order to get better numbers. It is not surprising, then, that newsworkers try to give the audience what it wants. One reporter's appraisal of the audience was shared by most of his colleagues.

And the thing is now when we get back to the station, is to keep it informative enough and short enough to not be offensive to the viewer who doesn't give a damn. We can spark his interest if I can start off with a flashy lead that will at least keep him there chewing his TV dinner and sipping his beer, til the next bigger news story comes up, we will have succeeded.

These images of the viewer, plus the pertinence of the ratings, inform what is done to "keep his interest." A reporter explained that the news should be what the viewer is interested in, and, in June 1972, he believed that the top things on people's minds were pollution, sex, racism, and the war in Vietnam. But he seemed unaware that people might be interested in these topics *because of* news reports.

If the numbers are too low, however, the organizational conclusion is that the viewers are not getting what they want. This is why "good" news means "good numbers." And this is why the Sales staff, Management, and newsworkers look to the ratings for indications of success and security. By the same token, reporters at Channel B considered the news coverage of their competitor,

Channel A. The influence of other stations vying for the same market influenced the operations of each station.

Competing Media

Channel B also exists in a media environment. In addition to several radio stations which broadcast news reports, the majority of news in 1972-1973 came from a morning and evening newspaper (owned by the same company), and another television station, Channel A (Altheide and Rasmussen, 1976). These other media, and especially Channel A, are important to Channel B's operation for at least three reasons:

(1) They may provide different or more current news reports than Channel B, and thereby question, challenge, or even contradict the latter's news report;

(2) other media are often regarded as more or less competent compared to Channel B, and Channel B's personnel evaluate their work vis-à-vis that of the other station;

(3) most importantly, Channels A and B compete for the same market.

How well a station does in these areas provides newsmen with a sense of what kind of a "job they are doing," and in some cases they become convinced that their organization is either inferior or superior to the competitor's. For example, Channel A advertised in *TV Guide* that its anchorman was the "fairest, most believable, most professional, and most respected TV news anchorman in Western City."

I will now briefly discuss each of the reasons listed above.

OTHER MEDIA PROVIDE A CHECK

Newsmen attend to the competition's news in order to determine what they have missed and whether their treatment of any given story was warranted. If there is agreement on what is newsworthy and if stories are treated similarly, then objectivity is achieved. Channel B occasionally monitored Channel A's newscast to see what was being covered and how much time was devoted to sports, weather, and world and national news. (This was given more significance since A led in the ratings.) In other words, newsmen assume that most newsworthy stories will be covered by most news media. To the extent that this occurs, there is not only a great deal of duplication, but news competence has been established. Those in charge of assigning stories to be covered take great pains to justify their omission of stories that other media will carry. This occurred at one station when the "desk" (i.e., the assignment editor) explained to the producer that he knew about a particular story "but just didn't think it was that big." He was thereby insuring his competence as a newsworker. Others explained to me that if several competitors routinely had stories they missed, then they would have to look at what kind of job they were doing.

OTHER MEDIA FORCE EVALUATION

The impact of the media environment on the station's competence follows from the first point but cuts a wider swath. Two areas commonly compared and evaluated are reporting and production techniques.

Reporting. Channel B's newsmen were convinced that they did a more professional job than the competition. This was especially apparent with investigative reports on sensational topics. A reporter's sources, or contacts, are crucial in these stories because many of these topics are covered up. To have good contacts implies that good reporting is being done.

Contacts tend to be more personal and unshared with competing media. This means that a reporter knows he is doing a good job if his contacts provide him with exclusive information. What is exclusive depends not only on the source, but also on the nature of the competition. If no one else is interested in the story, a certain flair is lost. To this degree, the snap of breaking a big story is muted if the competition doesn't compete.

This occurred with an investigative report on corruption at an international border crossing. Channel B's top reporter "scooped" the other station about forthcoming indictments and future investigation plans. He was quite surprised when he learned that the competition was not interested in the story even though the investigation would continue for several months, and a great deal of bribe money had already changed hands. Channel B's top man used the lack of interest as an indication of incompetence. He "couldn't believe that no other news media picked up the story after our series." He felt that perhaps one of the cameramen had put his finger on it, that "this town is so parochial, that they [Channel A] figure . . . it is 'his story' and therefore leave it alone, rather than competing or even contradicting the other guy."

On another occasion this reporter talked about Channel A's "big gun," their top reporter. After reminding me that this person got all the top stories, he added that it was remarkable why he didn't do better reporting.

> [He] never really gives comments; what he does is string together a bunch of facts. He doesn't really do reporting in the sense [B's reporter] does, but rather, engages in getting different points of view, and certain things he feels are facts. But he never really goes after something, with an eye on exposing or making a point about something [my paraphrase].

When referring to a story that Channel B was doing on high school violence, this reporter alluded to the way the competition would handle it: "[He] would get a few points of view, but wouldn't do any real investigation."

Production Techniques. It was well understood by newsmen at both stations that Channel B's production was better in virtually every respect. The many facets of production can be included under two subcategories: equipment and material, and individual competence. The two are somewhat related in that good equipment enables one to also be competent in one's work, but they are often quite distinguishable.

If the tools one works with cannot be trusted to respond when needed (e.g., if a switch is faulty), or to produce the quality a cameraman has in mind (e.g., if a lens has an abberation and is virtually useless), individual talents are not as readily demonstrated and the final product may fall below professional standards. Because of these considerations, newsmen take equipment problems in general, and faulty camera and sound systems in particular, as epitomizing a station's lack of concern with quality news. They realize that the best equipment costs a great deal of

money (sound cameras start around $6,000), and that local oper-
ations simply cannot afford to outfit each cameraman with the
latest word in cinematography. Nevertheless, many of their ex-
pectations can be traced to other local stations they have worked
with, known about, or talked with others about. This was reflected
in a conversation between two cameramen about a visit from a
Hawaiian colleague.

> He said that over there they [cameramen] all have "scopics" [a popu-
> lar type of camera] and they never run the processor [i.e., the film
> processor—an undesirable job]; they have a guy to do it. Their cars are
> marked and they can use them for pleasure.

The most immediate source of comparison was Channel A.
Their cameras (like Channel B's) were powered by batteries if
no electricity was available. The cheap battery system was constantly a source of trouble. On several occasions, I saw Channel
A's reporters "lose interviews" when the camera would not roll
due to a power problem. Members of both stations acknowledged
that B's equipment was better, although B's reporters, too, were
not free of problems. In one instance, a cameraman rushed to
the scene of a "cat rescue." As he focused his sound camera, the
cat leaped toward the lens; the cameraman hit the "button but
nothing happened, so I missed it all." On the whole, however,
these "screw-ups" were usually made tolerable with the comment,
"just remember, it's not as bad as Channel A."

Newsmen at Channel B repeatedly looked to their competition
as a prime example of how *not* to do the news. They had in mind
the poor quality of equipment, but also the lack of individual
care or precision in framing a picture, improper editing, and poor
coordination between technicians to have "it come off okay." In
fact, another researcher, who was working at Channel A, was
allowed—and encouraged—to actively participate in editing film
for a documentary. Channel B never permitted me to do this,
even though I was on good terms with several cameramen. On
several occasions employees of the competing station openly
admitted that their production was lousy and that many of their
people were "unprofessional" and "careless." The point is not
that Channel B's staff was never "sloppy," but rather, that it was

recognized by members of both stations that B's production was on the whole much better.

But this is only one measure of quality work; another is the ratings.

I already mentioned that Channel B trailed Channel A in news ratings by nearly two to one. The meaning of "having the numbers" is reflected in the words of one Channel A reporter:

> It doesn't really matter what kind of news is broadcast—we could have the worst news and the worst working conditions, but *all that really matters is how we look in the ratings*. That's what management looks at in the meetings; that's what's important. We're beating the competition two to one in the ratings, so our news must be good.

The most important point is that the media in Western City consider their competition. Furthermore, this is defined by the size of the market, or approximately 450,000 households. These local stations do regard the networks and other affiliates as models of change—e.g., altering formats, reporting style, and the like—but they are much farther removed, both geographically and practically. The observation that they seemed to operate in a more or less self-contained environment was largely corroborated by a newsman in a nearby city and another market: "Those guys [newsmen in Western City] have always lived in our shadow and have never really had to push for their bread and butter."

He meant that they were not competitive and were obviously not considering the larger station as part of the broader context in which they worked. Indeed, some of Channel B's newsmen agreed that their news was inferior to that found in larger operations. The implication is that those who worked in smaller markets were less competent. This came up when a newly hired reporter was held up to a cameraman as a "hotshot." The cameraman replied, "Yeah, if he's so hot why ain't he with the networks or in Northern City?"

Those who worked at Channel B were aware of the "small time" operation which paid their bills. But the competition with Channel A was part of the environment which gave them the occasional urge to do a better job which made them winners or losers in the rating race. In this way, the other station provided an added meaning to their tasks, which was also true of the station's community ties.

Community Context

Channel B's news focused on events in a confined area, and its signal reached nearly 450,000 homes. In the next chapter, I will show how various news sources in this "market" contribute to what is presented as news. The present focus is on the influence of certain people and institutions within Western City.

Unlike network bosses, most local station managers have close and frequent contact with newsworthy people. There are two reasons for this. First, there are usually similar political interests between the station managers and local politicians and business people. Epstein (1973: 56) observes that most have conservative sympathies. This was also true at Channel B, Channel A, and a half-dozen other stations I have experience with. Second, the personal contacts are not only based on self-selection among friends who travel in the same social circles, but powerful decision makers tend to court those who can provide information outlets to the public. By the same token, the station managers benefit from these associations.

This was true of Channel B's top man, who was one of the state's most prominent Republicans. Channel B's news director, who worked very closely with the station manager saw himself as a "king maker." He helped his man win the mayoral contest and indicated a continuing interest in his political future. It is my impression that the news director and station manager promoted news coverage of this politician in order to provide publicity. The news director ordered his crews to cover the mayor in numerous situations, and despite efforts to be uncooperative by reporters and camera operators, the mayor succeeded in receiving a tremendous amount of news coverage.

The most blatant support by the "king maker" and the station manager came from editorials. The justification for editorials is to perform a community service—and thereby fulfill an important Federal Communications Commission (FCC) requirement—by expressing "the views of management on important issues." Channel B editorials tended to focus on issues compatible with the mayor and other favorite sons. Few studies of the editorial process are available, but one study by Frank Wolf (1972) showed that most network affiliates presented nearly eight editorials annually. Channel B averaged nearly one editorial a week. Editorial opinions about ballot propositions appeared almost daily one month prior to balloting. Like most other affiliate stations, Channel B never endorsed a political candidate, although the mayor's position was solicited and written as "the views of management."

The news director was in charge of the station's editorials, despite a tradition of keeping management out of the news. On one occasion he admitted that the editorials on upcoming ballot propositions were how he would vote, although the credit for writing the opinions was always given to an "editorial researcher." The official explanation of the editorial process that was given to survey researchers inquiring about Channel B's editorial policy was that the station manager, the news director, and an editorial researcher had a hand in selecting topics and choosing the station's position. In fact, however, the editorial researcher was designated as an "editorial nigger" by his colleagues. He saw himself as "just a flunky around here." His task was to do the management's bidding and write what they told him. Generally, he would be told what position Channel B would take on an issue, and his task was then to find supporting material or "evidence." When the station manager read the editorial on camera he would often state, "our careful research shows . . ."

One example illustrates the compatibility of the Management's thinking with the mayor's position. In May 1971, Channel B editorialized against a review of the city charter proposed by the old mayor. They said,

If there is confusion and suspicion about city government, as the mayor indicates, it apparently results from the indictments returned against several city officials last year, not from the basic form of government. That should not be cause for us to consider scrapping our present city charter. Channel B believes another charter review is not needed at this time and recommends a 'no' vote on Proposition Z.

But the election of the new mayor led to a change. By the special election in November 1973, Channel B not only supported charter review but editorialized in favor of a proposition which would fundamentally change the council-manager form of city government to a mayor-council-manager form. The general result would be to establish a "strong mayor."

In another editorial, on model cities, Channel B lauded the city's highest official: "Channel B applauds Mayor _____'s apparent philosophy in reducing the executive committee to a more actionable size." Generally, the mayor's programs were more subtly supported through editorials and a weekly half-hour "Discussion" show hosted by the news director.

One editorial criticized county officials' reluctance to cooperate with the mayor: "Channel B hopes the [officials] will compromise its own apparent stubbornness and work from within the system." The same stubborn officials were berated several weeks later on "Discussion." After presenting filmed interviews of a disagreement between the mayor (as representing the "city") and his detractors (as representatives of the "county") regarding who should have veto power over proposed federal programs, one newsman made it clear that he wasn't certain why the federal government selected the city over the county. Nevertheless, the news director persisted:

> I am still not satisfied with the labor department's rationale. In talking to them now, did you get the impression ... that the choice of the city over the county was because they didn't think the county was capable of handling the job?

The reporter's negative answer ended the discussion.

The linkage to the mayor was one way the community context influenced news reports, but there were others. Channel B, like many local stations, cooperated with police departments, and submitted unsubpoenaed film for use as evidence against demonstrators. In addition to good public relations, assisting the police also provided good news stories. Two of Channel B's employees were reserve police officers, which meant that they could attend briefings about planned "drug busts" and then be on the scene when "it came down," as cars came screaming up to residences, as "suspects" fled in panic and were tackled, arrested, read their rights, and then packed off to jail. Meanwhile, Channel A, while tops in the ratings, lagged in police contacts. They would not get the story until they heard it over the police radio monitor. But one of their camera operators had excellent relations with an FBI agent which proved to their competitive advantage on other occasions.

These contacts were hotly criticized by the reserve officers' colleagues. They felt that such relations compromised their loyalties and were concerned that news reporters would cease to be trusted and might even be attacked by those they filmed and reported about. This was especially true of antiwar demonstrators who believed that their pictures would be used by police officials. On several occasions I became very anxious that someone would brand us all as snitches who were "filming for the pigs." In fact, police officers began masquerading as news cameramen in order to obtain the pictures they wanted. Most of this did not sit well with many news agents. The mixed loyalty of the reserve police officers-cameramen became apparent one evening, when one man was assigned to accompany a reporter to a rock concert where trouble was expected. When the disgruntled audience and police officers began exchanging rocks, the camera operator became a reserve officer, put down his camera, and began moving patrol cars into position!

Its relationship with the police promoted Channel B's share of dramatic film stories, but also discouraged serious efforts to investigate and follow-up reports about police corruption, brutality, and incompetency. The same was true with most investigative reports: They were virtually nonexistent, although some subjects were investigated. For example, Channel B's award-winning report on corruption among immigration officials led to several indictments. However, they failed to follow up a beginning report on violence in several of the district's high schools. As their top investigative reporter began filming interviews with the victims and their parents, the superintendent of schools, who was a friend of the news director and station manager, put a stop to it. The story was "killed," the reporter explained, not by overt censorship—that was too controversial—but by "reassigning" the story to a less aggressive reporter. A few experiences like this encourages a more innovative reporter "to not give a shit [and] just do my job."

Summary

An important part of the news process is the environment in which it exists. Among the relevant contributors to Channel B's news were commercialism and the ratings. The push to obtain the largest share of the audience in order to add to the station coffers through advertising revenue promoted an entertaining style to "capture the numbers." This in turn led to a cynical view of the audience—stupid, incompetent, and unappreciative. From this perspective, viewers threaten the "success" of the news operations and, even more directly, may influence decisions to hire and fire newsworkers.

The battle for the largest share of the audience is significant for the competition. If they are losing, then you are doing a good job; but if they are ahead in the numbers game, then your work is suspect. Another contribution of the competition was to provide a comparison for workloads, equipment repair, and the work situation in general.

The competition was one part of the environment that influenced how newsworkers performed, but the political environment helped shape the content of news reports. In Western City the mayor and other officials hobnobbed with Channel B's Management. Their causes were promoted mostly through editorials, although news stories were also selected to give their version. The same was true of the police, and of most institutions. Placing the news operation in its environment lays the foundation for moving on to discuss how news is defined, selected, and organized.

Chapter 3

ORGANIZING FOR NEWS

News reports reflect the organization which produces them. This chapter examines the division of labor in Channel B's newsroom, and connects these roles to the news sources and technology used by newsworkers.

Channel B's news department has a staff of twenty-five—reporters, cameramen, anchormen, producers, writers, researchers, sportscasters, and two secretaries. The main staff is male except for one female reporter. The ties of the newsroom to the remainder of the station flow through the news director who is responsible to the station manager. Second in command is the producer (also assistant news director). He is followed by the assignment editor (e.g., the "desk"). While the news director, producer, and "desk" run the operation, the soldiers of the newsroom are the reporters and cameramen, who in turn are backed by an editorial researcher and several writers who occasionally fill in as producers or occupy the desk. All of this requires organization.

The organization of news promotes numerous problems. For one thing, there are different goals to be fulfilled by various parties to the news process. For another, these interests sometimes conflict. However, the overriding goal is to have enough material for the evening newscast. If this does not occur, then lucrative commercials will not be shown, ratings and revenue will drop, and jobs may be lost. While all workers are aware of this practical problem, considerable resentment is apparent when, for example, reporters and camera operators are forced to compromise their criteria of excellence and competence, with commercialism. The different perspectives on news are illustrated with a brief examination of the news director and producer at Channel B. More extended treatment will be given the assignment editor who selects stories for coverage, and the reporters and camera operators who cover these events.

The News Director

The news director is in charge of the news operation. He is responsible to the station manager in virtually all stations and, in most stations, oversees daily routines and serves as a public relations coordinator. I already mentioned how the news director was involved in editorial policies and promoting local politicians. This interest, along with his gruff and suspicious manner, earned him few friends among his subordinates.

Few of Channel B's employees knew exactly what the news director did. Most agreed that his time was spent looking busy, appearing important, and engulfing himself in trivia such as calls from viewers, work scheduling, and the like. But he demanded respect, and he used his authority to coerce those not on "his side." For example, he would cut the overtime of reporters and camera operators who were out of his favor. To put it mildly, he was not well liked and was regarded as incompetent by everyone I had contact with during my one-year stay in the newsroom, including his friends. His personal relationships with people were disastrous, but one of the main reasons he was so detested could be traced to his toleration of the producer and the assignment editor (desk). Their work created daily problems for the news crews, who in turn would blame the news director for putting up with their ineptness.

The Producer

The producer is primarily responsible for coordinating the work of the news director, the assignment editor, and the reporters and cameramen. He is in charge of putting the show together by deciding what stories will come first, second, and so on, as well as how much time each will be allocated. The producer at Channel B did his job by filling the show according to the format.

THE FORMAT

Channel B's format included world and national news, local news, sports, and the weather report. These items, plus an occasional "comment" and "perspective" made up the newscast. Of course, commercials were interspersed throughout. Once the format was set (and it changed several times in an attempt to raise the ratings), the task was to fill in the "show order," or the order in which news items will appear. A "show order" for Monday, January 31, 1972, is presented in Table 1 as an example.

The producer's main responsibility is to make certain there is enough material to fill the one-hour newscast, although there is always leeway for ad-libs, slow talking, etc. The format pretty well lets him know how much time needs to be filled. For example, the show order indicates that nearly 14 minutes are accounted for by commercials; another 2 minutes are required for "teases" and "tossess"; the sports and weather are alloted 5 and 4 minutes, respectively. The format also calls for a standard 3:30 for "world and national news." This totals to nearly 29 minutes of news. The remaining 25 to 30 minutes will be filled with local film stories, the "perspective," "live items," and video packages provided by the network.

If the local news is particularly slow, the wire services can always be counted on for "live items" to be read (without film) by the anchorman. If the producer decides that there are holes to fill, he always has a stack of wire copy which can be rewritten to standard lengths, usually from 20 to 45 seconds. The number of live items varies from two to ten, depending on how much time needs to be filled.

Another way to fill holes is the network News Program Service (NPS) video "feed" which provides monthly "features," or less

Table 1: A Show Order

Subject	Length	
1. Open	:30	(e.g., "This is the Channel B early news")
2. Headline Tease	:30	
3. World and National	3:30	
4. Tease	:07	(e.g., "more on this in a moment")
commercial	:30	
commercial	:30	
commercial	:30	
5. Film Story A	2:00	
6. Live Item	:30	
7. Film Story B	1:00	
8. Live Items	:45	
9. Tease	:07	
commercial	:30	
commercial	:30	
commercial	:30	
commercial	:10	
10. Tease	:10	(e.g., "and now we'll find out why bread costs so much")
11. Agc. and Stox	4:00	
12. Live Items	:45	
13. Tease	:07	
commercial	:30	
commercial	:30	
commercial	:30	
commercial	:10	
14. Live Items	:45	
15. "Perspective" Toss	:10	(e.g., "Doug Smith has some thoughts on this")
16. "Perspective"	3:00	
17. Tease	:07	
commercial	:30	
commercial	:30	
commercial	:30	
commercial	:10	
18. Sports One	3:00	
commercial	:30	
commercial	:10	
commercial	:60	

Table 1: A Show Order (Continued)

Subject	Length	
19. Sports Two	2:00	
commercial	:30	
commercial	:30	
commercial	:30	
20. Film Story C	:30	
21. Film Story D	1:50	
22. Film Story E	:30	
23. Film Story F	1:30	
24. Film Story G	:30	
25. Tease	:07	
commercial	:30	
commercial	:30	
commercial	:30	
26. Film Story H	1:30	
27. Live Items	:30	
28. Film Story I	2:00	
29. Live Items	:30	
30. Tease	:07	
commercial	:30	
commercial	:30	
commercial	:30	
31. Live Item	:30	
32. Weather Toss	:07	(e.g., "in a moment we'll find out if tomorrow is a good day for a picnic")
33. Weather, National	2:00	
commercial	:60	
34. Weather, Local	2:00	
35. Close	:30	(e.g., "thanks for being with us; Bill will return with more Channel B news at 11:00")

timely stories each day at 3:00 p.m. This filler enables affiliate stations to cover any time surpluses, e.g., the scheduled news is lacking several minutes. This will commonly occur because one anchorman may read too fast, that is, faster than three seconds per line of copy, or one or more stories may have to be scrapped because tape machines or projectors may malfunction. For these reasons NPS is often a lifesaver. By the same token, this news source is relied on when other news is not forthcoming. This is more true of the noon news since film crews generally do not have time to cover local stories, process film, and have it ready for the noon show. Consequently, film stories are at a premium and the time is often filled with NPS features.

In order to insure having enough film stories available, selected pieces are stacked nearby. At any time the producer may rush in from the booth and ask a writer, "What have you got?" Several alternatives will be suggested, and the producer will then choose one—e.g., seminaries advertising in *Playboy* to attract recruits. In this way, the packaging of the news show can be routinized.

The producer was also expected by many coworkers to allocate time to each item in the show order according to its importance as a news story. He seldom did this, but tended to arbitrarily assign time to a story without knowing much about the content. On other occasions, he would grant someone's request to "give me two minutes" without seeing the film or talking to the reporter about what he had. This practice, plus the organizing aid of the format, permitted him to quickly complete his daily work. Not everyone felt the job was as complete as it should be. One reporter explained that generally, "he's already put the show together by 11 o'clock, so that he doesn't have to do anything the rest of the day."

The producer spent very little time evaluating the merits of any story, and never did I see him suggest a better way to do it. Even though newsmen might not have taken such advice kindly, they felt that it should be forthcoming. Some cameramen, for example, became so convinced that no one cared about their work that they intentionally started "doing as little as possible." One cameraman boasted that he was going to see just how bad his work could get before anybody would say anything. Most importantly, newsworkers felt the producer should recognize this shoddy work. When he never even expressed an interest, his competence was further jeopardized.

However, newsworkers realized that he wasn't the only one responsible for "the way things are done around here." The assignment editor who selected and assigned news stories probably touched them most directly.

The Assignment Editor ("desk")

The assignment editor is in charge of selecting stories from the various news sources, e.g., wire services, newspapers, press releases, and telephone calls.

The producer arranges news items according to the format, but the desk is responsible for providing the content. He knows that five to ten local film stories lasting from 1:00 to 2:30 each will be required to fill the local portion of the newscast. In other words, providing enough news is a problem he shares with the producer.

The concern with having enough news influences the news process in several ways. While news will ideally be new, organizational considerations preclude too much newness. A series of deadlines require careful scheduling in order to have enough news for the 5:00 p.m. newscast. It takes approximately 45 minutes to process film (before the "minicam"); another 15 to 30 minutes to do a marginally good job of editing; driving time to and from stories, and the time actually required to cover the news event. This is why most stories must be known about hours (or days) before the actual newscast.

The desk can only select stories he knows about. Since he needs to be able to assign crews, he must have prior knowledge about newsworthy events. For these reasons he relies on certain news sources for the majority of news stories. Among the dominant sources for Channel B were press releases, the local newspaper, various radio monitors (e.g., fire, police), and the wire services (cf. Epstein, 1973: 142). In addition to their almost constant availability, they could also be trusted because they were institutionally verified. For example, if a press release stated that a local military commandant would be awarded a medal at 2:00 p.m. on Thursday, the chances were very good that the event would occur. More to the practical point, chances were good that the desk could assign a crew to cover this presentation, and therefore include it in a newscast. To this extent, planned and scheduled news is good news.

Table 2 presents a brief overview of the sources for the stories contained in the show order (Table 1). Eight of eleven stories presented on the evening newscast (Monday, January 31, 1972)

Table 2: News Items and News Sources

Source	Topic	On News?	No. on "Show Order"
1. personal	"Perspective"	yes	15
2. wire	Bus. & Agr. Report	yes	11**
3. *	Blimp Feature	no	——
4. *	Clothespin Feature	***	——*
5. press rel.	Prof. Growth Day	no	——
6. several	Film Story H	yes	26
7. press rel.	Feature	no	——
8. press rel.	Film Story G	yes	24
9. press rel.	Film Story I	yes	28
10. press rel.	Film Story B	yes	?
11. press rel.	Film Story E	yes	22
12. press rel.	Film Story F	yes	23

*I was unable to learn the exact source, but a press release is probable.
**These stories were filmed on Friday, January 28, 1972.
***This story appeared on the news, February 1, 1972.

were known about on the previous Friday (January 28, 1972)—
i.e., not counting "world and national." The desk's "future file,"
(i.e., a depository for potential news stories) contained thirteen
press releases, three newspaper clippings, a few "live items," and
several notes. From these sources, the desk drew up the "beat
sheet" or tentative news schedule for Monday's news. Table 2
illustrates the importance of what is included in the beat sheet
for future news. The source, item, and whether or not it was on
Monday's news reflect such prescheduling. The importance of
certain news sources which facilitate scheduled coverage extends
to the amount and nature of news. For example, the news varies
by time of day (evenings are slow) day of the week (weekends
are slow), and month of the year (summers are slow). The nature
of news is also affected—for example, more press conferences are
held during the week. These fluctuations in news can be directly
traced to the dominant sources of news. The relationship between
the two can be illustrated with radio monitors.

RADIO MONITORS

Six radio monitors hang in Channel B's newsroom and adorn
most news operations. Included are monitors for police, sheriff,

fire, and the highway patrol. These are the main source for "spot news," or unplanned, "breaking," and more spectacular news, such as homicides, suicides, burglaries and fires. Each day's newscast has one or two of these stories which are learned about by certain police code designations. For example a robbery is a "211," a burglary is a "459," homicide is a "187." There are nearly 100 additional codes which are usually not recognized since they are not considered newsworthy—e.g., illegal parking, "586." Some of the different codes news agents use as part of their own radio communication with the station—e.g., "10-19" (return to station), "10-7" (out of service), and "code 7" (eating).

These codes represent a small portion of the ever-present radio clatter, but tend to be disproportionately selected and presented as dramatic stories involving police. Spot news stories are not broadcast with the intention of presenting such views, but rather, because they are deemed newsworthy, vis-à-vis other available news stories. Spot news represents the drama, suddenness, and "on the spot" news coverage with which newsmen associate news. Another important reason is that it is convenient, especially on evenings and weekends, and is commonly "all that is available." As one reporter explained, "Night news is a little different from day news . . . there is a lot more crime."

There are several reasons why there is likely to be more crime news in the evenings and weekends. First, the radio monitors are less audible during the day than on evenings and especially weekends. The importance of being able to hear this news source, especially when several sources clatter for attention, cannot be too strongly emphasized. One evening while I was riding with a cameraman and a reporter, a call for an ambulance ("11-41") came over the police monitor. The cameraman correctly remarked that "they probably wouldn't even hear it at the station," and therefore would not dispatch anyone to the scene.

A second reason why monitors are more relied on for evening and weekend news is the absence of an assignment editor. He doesn't work because there are few weekend news sources which permit scheduled coverage; little occurs which the desk may learn about from press releases, newspaper clippings, and the like. Also, since less time is available for the newscast (one-half hour at 5:00 and 11:00), there is less need to diligently search for news.

Consequently, more police-related stories are likely to appear on weekends. However, this news source only supplements the more organized and scheduled pieces derived from press releases which permit news to be planned and scheduled.

From the desk's perspective, news is defined in terms of scheduling, rather than of substantive importance. The interest in filling the show is illustrated by an exchange between a reporter and the desk about a coupon story.

Rep: Bay River VFW Jr. Unit of the Ladies Auxiliary; well, that blows 15 seconds of our story; how much do we have left (laughs)?

Desk: (laughs) You've got a lot today because it's all very slow. Uh, do a piece on what they're coming up with the coupons for, where they could send them, and then we'll put the phone number on a super on the screen, about 2½ minutes; it'll be a cute little interview.

Rep: I'll stand up to my waist in coupons.

Desk: Yeah, that'll be cute. .... They have already gotten a kidney machine for people in need here in Western County; they're doing a lot of good things, and they're trying to get a 66 passenger bus for some retarded kids, so you know, *it's not a news story, but.* ....

The concern with time is also why stories for the 5:00 p.m. news may be assigned as late as 3:00 p.m.—e.g., "[Producer] has a two-minute hole in his show to fill."

The evening newscast is filled with stories from the most available news sources—e.g., press releases and newspapers. One cameraman's opinion of these sources is obvious.

C.M.: Those son-of-a-bitches aren't getting any press releases, they don't know what to do otherwise.

D.A.: Is that right?

C.M.: That's right, they depend so much on those damn press releases coming in there and telling them, you know, to go here and do this, that they have developed no outside sources for news.

In several instances, reporters' suggestions for stories went unheeded until they appeared in the newspaper several days later. Nevertheless, filling a daily newscast requires using such sources, especially since the amount of news varies by month of the year, day of the week, and time of day. A reporter explained that the ratio of bad stories to good ones is about 10 to 1:

Rep: Only because there's such a large number of reporters at the station, you see, that cuts your odds immediately. I mean, if I were doing all the stories and could take my pick of what I covered, then I'm sure things would be highly improved, but I'd also be working my butt off, but uh, as far as the good stories are concerned ... I'm not saying that we don't get good stories from the station, it is just that the various reporters don't always get them.

This suggests that a reporter's and a camera operator's work is also affected by the assignment of stories.

The nature of the news sources and the desk's editorial whims provides a fertile organizational context for favoritism, privilege, and politics. As one newsman put it,

What we're talking about is, you'll hear pretty much—you know, and then it'll go in degrees—the same gripes in all stations, it's just that, it's just really bad in our situation that we have an assignment editor who can't think past his nose, and then *he's playing politics with all the other guys in the fucking station. I think I told you before that we've got to play politics,* you know, and give the stories, like he goes, okay, the top story of the day goes to such and such, and he works only with so and so, and this kind of crap gets old after a while.

The dearth of good stories plus the necessity of assigning a certain number in order to have the nightly news gives rise to an informal "fucking pecking order." In fact, "insiders" were claimed to get "more than their share" of desirable assignments.

It depends on who you know, whether or not one guy wants to do the story or not. Like right here, ["desk"] was going to send [cameraman] who was near the station over there to do it, but he changed his mind. So instead you send a two-man crew out to the other side of town rather than send a one-man crew who doesn't want to do it.

The "leftovers" go to the "outsiders."

Some reporters, ["desk"] will give them something to do, and they'll say, shit, I'm not going to do that. Give it to somebody else . . . and unfortunately the camera assignments are given to somebody else—me.

Not surprisingly, a relationship was felt to exist between the quality of a story and "who gets it."

C.M.: You know that when he puts the two of us together what the hell the story is.

D.A.: Are you guys bad luck when it comes to stories?

Rep: I don't know. It seems like ["desk"] sets [cameraman] and I up to cover all the crap; wouldn't you say that (referring to C.M.)? Primarily he knows we'll, you know, he does it, because he knows we won't give him a lot of shit; we'll just go out and do the job.

C.M.: He doesn't have any balls to tell the other guys to do it because they'll give him some static, [e.g.] "fuck you, ["desk"]."

This animosity suggests that there is far from perfect agreement about what newswork is and how it should be pursued. Moreover, many of these differences can be traced to disjunctions between the organization and reporters and cameraman. As one reporter put it, "It is like we were talking this morning, we're not used, and then when we're used, we're misused." Another newsman observed,

Like, you know [cameraman] and I get into arguments and we get over them; [another cameraman] and me get into arguments and we get over them. The thing of it is that we are in a supposedly very creative field and you have to let the guy express his creativity. You know, I can't stifle the photographer any more than he can stifle me, *but a lot of times because of the way that we're working and the way we're being assigned, we're being stifled by our own company.*

Such statements suggest that reporters and cameramen have a different outlook about news.

Reporters

A reporter's work begins after commercial, scheduling, and other problems have been solved (cf. Tunstall, 1972). A TV journalist's task is to find something newsworthy in events which have been selected for scheduling and other practical reasons. A report explained:

> I realize that the people I do work with are expecting a certain thing, so what I do is I try to read what other people are looking for and that's what I give them.

I noted above that press releases play a big part in local news coverage. While this routine news source solves the desk's problem by providing enough stories to fill the day's show, problems are created for reporters since most press releases announce press conferences or talking heads. According to one reporter.

> There are some things you can't do anything with. That's the majority of our stories. . . . You do an intro, and then into your talking head, and maybe B-roll [silent film] to break up the film.

From a reporter's perspective, his problems are compounded by those persons responsible for the kind of assignments he gets. "We've got an assignment editor who doesn't think past his fucking nose; a producer who doesn't think; a news director that doesn't know how."

The organizational interest in scheduling and predicting future news coverage, plus the format which calls for a half-dozen short and entertaining reports, creates a problem for reporters. It is partially solved by predefining what is important about an event and then using this as the basis for a story. *The capacity to approach events from one dimension and then show their significance by constructing a narrative account with a beginning, middle, and end is what I refer to as the news perspective.* Chapters 4, 5, and 6 present the use of this perspective in selected local and national stories. And in Chapter 7 I will emphasize what I now only allude to: *The news perspective fundamentally distorts most events it is presumed to illuminate.* The immediate task is to show the utility of predefined "angles" in news stories.

THE "ANGLE"

The reporter's task is to report what is newsworthy about an event. The "angle" facilitates placing unique occurrences in a

broader context and, in a sense, rendering "meaning by association." The relevance of the "angle" is suggested in this reporter's
comment.

Rep: We go out and we cover a story and we can say John Blow held up a
bank at 4th and Market St. and escaped with $14,000, police are
continuing the investigation . . . blah! Whereas, a bank robber, you
know, a bank robber robbed a bank at 3rd and A St.; this is the 14th
time this bank has been robbed; the teller who handed the money
over was Mrs. so and so who comes from another job at such and
such, a place where she had been robbed 4 times; her reaction to
this robbery was that it was unique in that she noticed this or that,
you know; *you make a story, you get hold of the basic foundation
and you build.*

Institutionalized angles like conflict are the most commonly used,
but other meaningful contexts are available. Angles may originate
in recent national developments, local happenings, and other concerns. An example of national developments providing a context
for the local side of the story was the release of the President's
Commission report on marijuana. An interview with an expert on
drug use was the obvious angle for the story. Channel B's coverage
of an airplane hijacking was also made more meaningful by the
broader national experience with this problem. Another example
of a national angle was put forth when a national political event
threatened to invade Western City. As Channel B's news director
put it on one telecast, "Security has become the name of the . . .
game in the wake of" such events as threatened assassinations and
the violence at the 1968 National Democratic Convention.

The local scene can also present appropriate angles. An investigative report on border corruption was repeatedly updated by
Channel B. More examples include stories about the good side of
young people in contrast to the "rash of demonstrations and un-
lawful behavior." If it weren't for the latter, the former would
have been less meaningful to the newsmen who covered these
stories. As one newsman explained about a story on volunteers
clipping "coupons" for a local charity:

Rep: We have had a good deal of inquiry about the good news, you know,
and so this could fall in that category—young kids who are involved
in something other than protests, and narcotics, and all that.

Still another source of angles is the newscast itself. A reporter covered a story on an alternative theory of creation set forth by a religious group. Even though he emphasized that the group's position was somewhere between Darwin and the biblical view, the reporter was instructed by the producer to include something about Bibles (although none were mentioned during the interview) because the "lead" to the next story was about "welfare cheaters swearing on a stack of Bibles." The concern to make the stories fit together thus became the angle for the story.

All of these angles are grounded in the reporter's sense of shared experience with fellow workers. Stated another way, particular events are related to a broader context, and it is the meaning of this wider framework which makes the story. While covering a demonstration at a local university, I asked the cameraman what was the most newsworthy thing. He replied,

> You mean, out of the whole thing? The flag coming down. The other stuff, I wouldn't have bothered. You know, I mean that's the school's business, but on the other hand, people have a right—they pay taxes— to know what's going on in their schools.

The topical angle of demonstrating a process was suggested with a story on weaving. The reporter explained, "They've already given me one lead because they call this a spin in, which is another demonstration, however it is different than the type we normally are accustomed to."

One story without an angle was an assignment to do two and one-half minutes on the local waterworks. The newsmen knew that since the story was assigned at 3:00 p.m., the intent was "to fill a hole" in the producer's show. Nevertheless, the reporter insisted that there was just "a bunch of double-talk in that script" and that "there was no new information." His problem was, "What do you say about water?" The story could have been more interesting had there been a rash of sickness attributed to water. However, since no such context was available, it had to stand on its own, and in the reporter's opinion, it didn't stand very well.

THE ANGLE AND EVIDENCE

Reporters select and present the content as evidence of the angle. The angle is the framework to which specific content will be nailed in order to tell a story. The important point is that the story is simply the format or medium through which a definition of an event—the angle—is presented. This means that the story is already pretty well set before they leave the station, although they must be certain to not make the mistake of "misconstruing" the story by letting the framework survive at the demise—and contradiction—of the content. A story on proposed alternatives to achieve more school integration illustrates the utility of the angle for content. As we left the station I asked the reporter,

D.A.: What the hell are you going to do?

Rep: Just barely give a background as to what these alternatives are; explain the story over [film] of kids, bless their little hearts, who have no say in the matter whatsoever, caught in the game of politics between their parents and the school board.

Thus, newsmen seek evidence which supports the story line.

Perhaps the clearest example of the use of evidence to support the story was a series done on massage parlors. The angle was illicit behavior: sexual exchanges, drug use, organized crime, and venereal disease. Masseuses were interviewed to obtain answers to these questions, and the film was edited to focus on these concerns.

Another example was the high school violence story. The angle pointed to undisciplined behavior in the public school, involving harassment of students and teachers to the point of stabbing. The evidence was well specified: a girl's cut arm. So important were the wounds for the story that the reporter feared they might heal prior to the scheduled interview. Also, he wanted the parents' reaction, and told them, "We'll talk about it and then put it on film." The idea was to have a dry run in order to make certain that everything pertinent to the story was included. It should be stressed, however, that not everyone involved in this story saw things the same way. During a discussion about this story, one newsman scoffed at the high school principal's version that the cut was merely a scratch. The newsman conjectured that the school didn't think it was serious enough unless a blood transfusion was needed. Another newsman cautioned against this interpretation, adding that the principal "probably didn't see himself as lying, but that he had a different interest."

One further example illustrates the problematic usage of evidence for stories. A reporter who was making a documentary on alcoholism used actors in addition to several alcoholics. When I asked him why he used actors, he explained that several alcoholics he interviewed "wouldn't talk about their problems," although, "they really loved to talk." He was concerned that they didn't provide the concrete statements which would illustrate his perception of the problems of habitual drinking. In fact, even the "genuine" alcoholic's comments were edited to articulate the story about the symptoms, misery, and solution to alcoholism.

As with the angle, the importance of evidence is most clearly seen when it is not available. This occurred when a reporter interviewed a lady who accused the Humane Society of vivisection—selling cats for scientific research. The interview prompted a Humane Society official to demand a retraction under threat of civil proceedings. The reporter explained the he knew "she was telling the truth, but couldn't prove it," and therefore ran the retraction.

USING THE ANGLE

Meaningful contexts for events are widely available and some are even institutionalized through news sources. For example, crime and destruction are learned about primarily from police and fire monitors. However, it is one thing to be available, but it is another to recognize and use the angle to the fullest extent. Often the reporter is not at fault, but his superiors "screw up." For example, a veteran political reporter who was assigned to report color (e.g., what people are wearing; the elevators not working) during election coverage, remarked, "On a night like tonight everything should be hard news; color is soft news."

More commonly, though, the reporter is assigned to cover the event and is relatively autonomous. This is where the reporter must "do something" with the story; he must "dig," "think," and "develop" the story as much as possible. Unlike the good

stories in which the reporter is less significant, most assigned coverage requires that the reporter do good work. A large part of this
work involves asking questions.

The reporter is primarily responsible for the story in an interview setting since there is little that is visual. Most reporters try
to have pre-interviews in order to get themselves together as well
as to ferret out what may be evidence for the story. One reporter
explained the utility of these "trial runs."

> You're limited to 2 minutes on camera right, so by letting him [the
> interviewee] ramble for his 20 minutes or one half-hour, how much
> ever time you can allot him, you can pick out the stuff that really is
> important. And by important, I mean whatever is important to the
> viewer at home because you're both people, at least that's what I, and
> I try to ask the types of questions that will mean the most to the viewer
> at home because let's say that I had some expertise in his field—which
> I do not—and I went in there and we both got the conversational plane
> up to a level that only 10 people out a million could understand what
> the hell we're saying; of what value is it then?

These questions are designed not only to elicit evidence but
also to be intelligible to the viewer.

> Rep: But I try to put myself, always put myself in the shoes of the guy at
> home. I say if the guy at home had the possibility of asking ques-
> tions, what would he ask you?

Another reporter discussed how difficult this is.

> I am more interested in what he is saying, not for reporting purposes,
> you don't remember everything you touch on; you don't remember
> what you're saying; you're not recording all of this for content, but
> just for strategy. A lot of times the photographer will listen and tell
> you to ask something else.

Reporters assume that the materials they get from an interview
will have to be edited and reduced. The reporter carves the raw
interview with his angle which enables him to tell a story with a
beginning, middle, and end. Once this is accomplished, he will
then work with the cameraman who will edit the film to portray

the reporter's version. One reporter explained how he reduced an interview with a scientist who reported new evidence supporting the "continental drift" theory of land mass location.

D.A.: Why do you use your recorder?

Rep: What I do with this is ... and I try to get the SOF [sound-on-film] ; I either put it down where we're talking or if you have a setup like [cameraman] does I plug it right into the system so that I get exactly what went on the film and I back my recorder up until I get to the point where we start to do the questioning. I write down the length of each of these answers after the first question. And that way, you know, I get an idea of how I am going to edit the SOF.

(The scientist discusses the major findings.)

Okay, now we've got 2:15 for that first answer, which is entirely too long.

D.A.: Okay, now, just one thing, now you didn't time your question; your question will just be narrated?

Rep: What you do when you write your introduction to the thing is you say, it is either in the track or 'I asked Dr. Smith' ... you know, if this does show the continental drift theory to be true. The reason I am saying that I may write it that way is because I think I am going to pick it up from the beginning of the answer, or the second part of the answer. So what I'll do now is I'll go back and retime that point and see how long that went.

D.A.: Okay, now, why will you pick that up there?

Rep: Because it's too long. I've got 2:30 for a story. That doesn't leave me any time to give the viewer any kind of background. I've got to have 15 seconds for [anchorman] just to get to me and the story. So, what I want to do is to try and find an area that runs about ... oh, 1:15 or 1:30; that gives me 15 seconds for him and 45 seconds for me to do a track and give the viewer a very condensed tight version of what went on today. And, that's why we try to edit this way. That's why it is such a valuable tool in that respect; so now I'll just back it [the recorder] up and take it from the second part of his answer of where I think we could do it. You have to be careful on this because you can't split it between a word. It has to be a natural pause of some kind. That sounds like a starting point.

(The scientist speaks.)

> This was the first answer which I think I can put into about 20 words. . . . So now I'll hold onto my stop watch until I get to the point where I think we should start and then I'll see how long it is.
>
> Okay, now, the answer from where I began runs 1:45 which is still too long. In this business 'would you like to do another leg (mission)?' [the question he asked the scientist] is an interesting kind of thing, so there are two things that I can do. I can leave out the business of drilling the deepest hole because you can also explain that very quickly, [e.g.] 'what did you find in the sediments.' Now I am going to go back and you'll see where I try to pick that up and see if I can save enough time to get the second question in or if I am just going to go with what we have.
>
> Okay, what I've done now is I have reduced a 3:30 interview down to 1:42 which I can live with; that cuts 12 seconds off my track. . . . I'll use about 12 seconds to introduce. That will give me 35 seconds of track in order to lay a ground rule for the thing. . . . And that's the way you do it, that's the way you get your SOF without ever having seen the film, then you pray it comes off without any problems. And if it doesn't, what you do is use B-roll to cover the track.

Reducing the story is important because of several organizational features noted previously. The problem with scheduling stories is also a deciding factor. How much play a story gets depends almost entirely on how much time is needed to fill. After the reporter reduced the interview, he added, "Now what I'll do is I'll go up and talk to the assignment editor and find out how fat he is for tonight; if he is very fat for that, then I am going to have to live with it."

A tape recorder can help obtain the evidence for the angle, but the reporter must ask the right questions to fully develop the story line. Several reporters agree with one newsworker's assessment of the importance of the angle.

D.A.: Do you get any kinds of feedback, like in terms of your reporting from other people in the station regarding what you do and so on?

Rep: Uh, from people at this station and people whose opinions I respect, they tell me that I am probably one of the fastest learning and aggressive reporters at this place, but again for people who don't

like me it would probably be the reverse; they think I am dumb, I
don't grasp the story, I don't know what the hell I am doing, *I am
always reporting on the wrong angle.*

One newsman was particularly critical of a colleague's reporting
on two stories. The first story was about sky marshals who were
being asked by the government to pay back expense money. The
most important aspects of the story, according to this reporter
were "how much money he had spent," "how much he had saved,"
"what had he done with the money," and so on. The original reporter explained that he had asked these questions, but didn't
think they were important enough to have in the story. So the
critical reporter added, "The most important questions were left
on the cutting room floor." He then described another "screw-
up." A member of a local Democratic Committee charged that the
GOP was offering prizes to registrars in order to encourage their
registration of more Republicans. The "super bad" reporter, however, didn't try to find out exactly what had gone on—that is, if
there was any basis to the charge—but chose instead to ask the
respective parties if the charges were true.

Another reporter was chastised for failing to ask more probing
questions in an interview with a former hoodlum. As we returned
to the station the interview was discussed.

C.M.: After you asked him about Bonnie and Clyde and how their lives were
glamorized, you should have asked him, why are you now negotiating to have your life made into a feature-length film (laughter)?

Rep: Yeah, [cameraman] is nasty, he thinks of all those nasty questions. . . .
I wish I would have thought of it (laughter).

The final example of "failing to ask the big question" was an
interview with an expert on acupuncture. The reporter failed to
inquire about the utility of this new treatment for Governor Wal-
lace, and thereby forfeited a nice opportunity to provide a more
encompassing national context.

Asking the right questions can be especially important in an
investigative report. While the press conference reporter often has
a prepared statement on which to base his questions, the investigative reporter must formulate his own angles. One implication of

this creativity is to not accept the stories and angles provided by official news sources. Channel B's top reporter explained that his idea of reporting involved not only getting both sides, but pushing the issue until you feel you can make some judgment about who is correct. Following the presentation of his award-winning investigative report on corruption at an international border, I jested about his "muckraking." He failed to see the humor.

Rep: Yeah, muckraking, hell. I'm really tired of that word. I'm really tired of journalists going up and just shooting interviews. That's really not journalism.

From this perspective, any newsman worth his salt should try to "cut the crap" and "push" officials and others who harbor such information.

Angles may also be used unwarrantedly to improve stories. Rosten's (1937: 259) observation that "the necessity of extracting startling angles from events, leads newspapermen to take liberties with the material and often do injustice to the facts." Rosten's point is well taken, but since the "facts" do not "speak for themselves," the use of news angles is necessary, inevitable, and unavoidable. However, we can be aware of these practices and thereby try to reduce their impact.

The intentional use of angles to distort stories was not a common practice at Channel B. Rather, newsmen used angles in other ways. Newsmen are supposed to subordinate personal interests to those which would make the story more meaningful and objective by using the appropriate angles. But occasionally one's personal interests would prevail, although cleverly masked by a presentation of the story as though the news angle were more central than the personal side.

There were several examples of presenting personal interests as though they were warranted by a larger concern. The news director was an avid scuba diver and frequently suggested that related stories be covered. One reporter was interested in sailing and made arrangements with a dealer to demonstrate and use his boats. Doing a story on sailing was not a condition of the arrangement, but since it would be good visually and would help promote the boat business, why not? However, the angle was the virtues of learning to sail, and avoiding certain dangers, and not directly his personal interest. Another newsman had an interest in opening a business which would receive financial backing from a racket ball baron. Presenting a story about "racket ball" was, to my knowledge, not part of any formal bargain, but was a nice way to reciprocate. The story was couched in terms of "leisure," a "rapidly growing sport," and a "great way to lose weight." Another story centered on an experimental school attendance plan where students would attend forty-five days of school and than have fifteen days off on a year-round basis. A reporter who covered the school beat became especially interested in this plan since his child was required to attend summer classes in facilities which the school board promised would be air conditioned, but were not. When the student complained, "Oh daddy, it's so hot at school," he began "research" on how well the plan was working. In the fall, he did a follow-up story on many teachers' unfavorable reactions, lack of money and facilities, and the like.

The importance of angles in a reporter's work is reflected in how stories are initially evaluated, how reporting is done, how individual newsmen are assessed, and how bias and misconstruing stories are recognized. We have also seen that reporters can use these understandings in ways beneficial to their own purposes, subject to specific whims, but still presentable as news. In utilizing this freedom they can shake the general context of meaning—to look for the news story in events—to its very foundations.

However, they are not alone in their work and must consider the perspectives of cameramen who accompany them to provide the content called for by chosen angles. I now switch focus to those who frame the context suggested by reporters.

Cameramen

The reporter's angle is often supplied through the cameraman's skill in filming and editing. A cameraman describes what he saw in "little frames" at a weaving demonstration.

C.M.: I am thinking in terms of film. . . . I saw the woman sitting there—the one big loom there—and I thought right away, I was thinking in a sequence. Okay, here's an establishing shot of her at the weaving thing through that bigger wheel and then move to her hands for a closeup, and then maybe cut in a shot of her face, of maybe her foot on the thing. You know, I was thinking in a sequence like that.

Their primary interest is to tell the story with film, although this must be achieved within the confines of the dominant organizational goals.

C.M.: What happens with the news is that they have to play the same game as the Lucy and the Carol Burnett Show. They've got to be not only informative, they've got to be entertaining too, so you have to do slick production.

And since news occurs on a daily basis, production must be standardized in order to cover the required number of stories.

C.M.: What's happening in news, ever since they had news on, everything is becoming standardized, [e.g.] one guy sits screen left, the other screen right, you know, and you shoot an over-the-shoulder shot of the interviewer, and you shoot reverse angles.

A cameraman's work is also limited by a tight budget which precludes shooting enough film for an optimum presentation. Channel B's cameramen shot a 3 : 1 ratio. That is, they used one-third of what they shot, although they preferred a much higher ratio. As one cameraman explained, "This station belongs to the budget school of photography."

While the amount of film shot is restricted, there is no doubt as to its purpose: to provide the evidence called for by the angle. This is why the reporter and camera operator practically always discuss how the event will be played.

Rep: Today we're going to be shooting this thing on the elementary school busing project. We're going to be talking about students. We'll be talking about ethnic balance so we have to show a certain amount of ethnicity in the film that we're shooting, so therefore we're going to shoot black students and white students.

EDITING

Editing can be done several ways. One is the cameraman's perspective, where he can edit "naturally" on film. The second mode of editing employs a cutter-splicer which dissects and integrates film, and a timer which transforms film footage into minutes and seconds. It should be emphasized that cameramen always film with the editing process in mind. A brief look at the wedding of filming to editing procedures clarifies how news content is susceptible to time constraints and the narrative form.

A cameraman can occasionally naturally edit a story. The deciding factor is the nature of the event, how long it lasts, and how it develops. The only example I encountered during my year at Channel B was a rescue story. Two city employees had been trapped in a cave-in. This spot news story was still in progress when the cameraman arrived, since it took time to get rescue equipment into position and carry out the necessary digging operations. The cameraman explained that it was a "spectacular story" and seemed very proud of it. I mentioned that it was cut very nicely. He told me that he didn't have time to edit it—that was the way it was shot, although some material had been deleted. Part of the problem was the ambulance took away one guy while the other one was still in the hole. He described how he ran to get a shot of the ambulance and then returned to the cave-in. I insisted that I thought that was a "cutaway" (i.e., shots to provide transitions between disconnected scenes), since it gave the impression of moving to another scene. He assured me that it was not, and that he ran with his camera to the other location. He added that "this type of thing is easy to film because it has a natural progression"—that is, one thing is naturally followed by another and therefore does not require rearranging on film.

Natural editing is not very common since few events are of such short duration and occur in sequences which permit telling the story without rearranging the action. The alternative is for the cameraman's edited version to be complimented by the editing bench. The basic process of physical editing is to reduce or rearrange film in order to transform the event into a story with a beginning, middle and end. This rearranging of film poses other problems, since almost every edit disrupts some natural filmed sequence. To splice these disruptions together usually heightens the "visual confusion" by creating "jump cuts" where activity occurs either out of sequence or with gaps. For example, one second the person's arms are over his head, and the next moment they are at his side without having moved on the screen. Another consequence of physical editing with sound-on-film is to create "blips" at each splice. For these reasons, edits must be covered with "cutaways" or "reversals."

Cutaways. The cutaway is a standard technique in television news film to give visual relief and avoid unprofessional jump cuts which invariably accompany any physical edit. The jump cut tells the viewer (newsmen believe) that something has been edited and that the film has been tampered with. The implication seems to be that if the film has been played with, so has the event, and perhaps objectivity has been breached. Thus, editing is deemed important not only for interesting visual effects but also to make the edited version seem as natural or as unedited as possible.

This understanding also informs how a story may be filmed. An experienced cameraman knows that he should film an event with editing in mind since the editing process transforms an event into news form (cf. Tuchman, 1969); to competently cover a news story is to capture an editable version of reality, and since he usually knows about the angle, he can "shoot the story." This means that a cameraman's job can be partially typified according to what is routinely filmed. This includes an "establishing shot" of the scene, such as a reporter and interviewee talking together. The second series of shots any cameraman frames depicts aspects of the event to be focused on in the story. The final consideration for filming an editable account of reality is cutaways to tie the previous film strips together.

Narrative form, continuity, and sequence. Visuals must be ordered to communicate. Narrative form achieves this organization by arranging film to correspond with a story line—a beginning, middle, and end. These must also be smoothly tied together in a continuous way, and it is this requirement which makes the use of cutaways an essential feature of television news. This becomes clearer if it is recalled that maximum lengths are imposed on news stories.

Continuity can only be maintained through the use of cutaways when an event is condensed, say, to a two minute report. If the beginning, middle, and end of the film story come from these segments of the events, the completed two minute story will consist not only of these three parts, but also cutaways to bridge the edited film. For example, while it may take five minutes for a crowd to walk from a plaza to a flagpole, the camera operator knows that he will have only a few seconds to show this, since the trek is less important than the arrival and the subsequent flag lowering.

A cameraman shot this story the following way. First, he got some footage of the crowd moving toward the flagpole. He then filmed them when they arrived, but also included footage of the flag before it was lowered. Next, he framed the flag being lowered, and later, raised again. The key pieces of film were the waving flag and its being lowered. The waving flag was inserted between the film of the crowd moving toward the flag and their arrival. The effect on the television screen was to create a sense of the crowd moving through time by first framing the crowd, then the flag, and then returning to the crowd. To go on film from the walking crowd to the flagpole would have been a jump-cut which is usually avoided.

The narrative form can be achieved only if the sequence is continuous and not obvious. Put differently, from a camera operator's (and editor's) perspective, editing must not be detected if good production is to be the result. This entails covering edits with either cutaways or B-roll—i.e., silent film. The former technique is most common in interviews.

C.M.: [Cutaways are] always a good thing to have in interview situations; it's a good thing to have an establishing shot, and then a reversal [i.e., a cutaway], of the people talking together, because when you get back [i.e., to the station], they say we only want 30 seconds of what this guy says . . . maybe he says something for 15 seconds that is not too hot but the last 30 seconds are, so we can edit the two 15-second segments together and cover that jump cut with B-roll or a reversal, where you see the reporter looking at the guy and then you can actually make the edit. Then you can go back and get the guy talking.

This technique is quite simple. The reporter will repeat several questions on camera after the interview is completed. Often the cameraman will change positions in order to give the impression of having two cameras. While the reporter generally repeats those questions more central to the story, the final decision will not be made until he confers with the cameraman. Assuming they have been given two minutes for the story, and since the lead-in may take fifteen seconds and the "close" (or "wrap") another thirty seconds, they have a minute and fifteen seconds for the inter- viewee's replies. If two comments are selected from different portions of the interview—as is commonly done—everything else is extraneous. In order to avoid jump-cutting, the interviewer's cutaway question will be inserted between the two replies. The idea is to create the impression that the conversation occurred in this sequence.

B-roll, or silent film, is designed for the same effect. Whereas the cutaway will usually be physically inserted between the two pieces of film with the interviewee's responses, B-roll is silent film on another roll which complements the sound-on film, or A-roll. For example, replies may be heard but silent B-roll will be seen. In the extreme cases, the A-roll can actually be converted to a voice track where the speaker will be seen and heard simul- taneously for only a few seconds. This will then be followed with his voice over the silent B-roll. This technique is likely to be used if many edits are made in the sound-on-film. The reason is simply that each edit must be covered in order to avoid jump-cuts; if there are a lot of edits it is easier to cover the whole thing with B-roll. One cameraman explained the use of this technique. The story was about a proposition regulating atomic power plants.

C.M.: So, we've got a city councilman down there who couldn't talk for more than 17 seconds without forgetting what the hell he was say- ing. He was one of the proponents of Proposition Z. . . . We shot the thing, and he would talk for 17 seconds and then, blaw, so each guy [i.e., the opposing sides] was given a minute and forty some seconds [to say his "piece"] but what we had to do is take and edit every one of his 17-second things that he could get out of his train of thought. . . . We put all those 17-second things together, and what we can do is, we can cover all these pauses with B-roll, wide shots, that are so far away you can never tell [i.e., that he is not actually saying what is heard].

Rep: Okay, but ostensibly what you have done is taken that from a film feed to a tape feed because it is no longer of any value filmwise because of the edits.

D.A.: I see.

Rep: The lip-sync [i.e., lips synchronized with words] would be totally off now.

D.A.: What do you do with that film then?

Rep: Okay, he runs that as an audio track and uses B-roll to cover.

D.A.: Oh, I see.

C.M.: With that wide shot through the trees, there is no way that you can see his lips; all you can see is his lips moving . . . he could be saying something besides what you're hearing.

D.A.: Oh, I see, that's the advantage of having the wider angle kind of thing.

Rep: But the edits from the original piece of film will reduce it to a sound track.

C.M.: You'll see this guy on the screen for about 17 seconds, long enough so they can put up his name . . . and then we'll go to the B-roll; they'll all be wide shots because . . . otherwise when we physically edit the film and the sound track, you know, you'll see his head in this position, and then in this position [i.e., a jump-cut]; you'll see his head jump where the edit was . . . you can't do things like that.

Another reason for shooting B-roll is to "cover your ass," especially if the reporter changes his mind or the desk wants the story to go longer. Using B-roll for insurance is apparent in the following comment, which also illustrates the different perspectives of reporters and camera operators:

C.M.: I always like to shoot a lot of B-roll for safety sake . . . because these guys [reporters] don't always know what they want. Just like when I started out shooting with [reporter], he told me we are going to use a lot of B-roll because we will only see these guys on the screen for maybe 20 seconds, long enough to get their names up and then we'll use B-roll over the whole time they're talking. . . . He gave me a list of about 50 different things to go out and shoot B-roll of, like power poles, plants, people watering lawns, appliance stores, traffic, flowers, and all these kinds of things. . . . So I just shot a lot of wide establishing shots, and shot reversals of these guys knowing . . . the way we had to edit that thing there was no way we could use all this other stuff, and that we would have to go more or less [with] wide establishing shots to cover all these physical edits we made. Sure enough that's the way it turned out . . . that's all we're going with now is the reversals.

Maintaining continuity does not necessarily distort the event; rather, the predefined angle, coupled with the narrative form, does. Most newsworkers agree that edited versions of events are more concise and more informative, especially since viewers are believed to have very limited attention spans. Just as verbatim transcriptions are not essential to derive essential meanings in everyday life, complete recordings are unnecessary to convey basic information which can generally be adequately summarized by a reporter. However, the technique of editing, and especially the notion that all edits must be covered if material is to be included, can alter the meaning. A reporter explained the difficulty.

Rep: I think it is oftentimes worth it to go ahead and have a jump-cut; if he says something important in the beginning, something important in the end, and he just meanders around through the middle, then take the middle out, throw it away, and whether you've got B-roll to cover it or not, run it that way. . . . I am not saying it should become a habit, I am just saying that it should be allowed.

D.A.: How can you wreck a story by trying to get rid of jump-cut, or how could you hurt a story?

Rep: I am saying that [the news director] allows no jump-cuts . . . on the air, so consequently *I have had to throw away whole segments of film that had some pretty good stuff in them because we didn't have B-roll, or something turns up that we didn't have anything to cover the jump-cut.* So I have had to take just the front half, or the back half and throw everything else away.

D.A.: I see. So you have the continuity. . . .

Rep: Yeah, the continuity was there but there was no B-roll to cover it.

D.A.: So, what you're saying is that what is continuous may not always be the most interesting.

Rep: Exactly.

The importance placed on the physical editing to convey the essential message while presenting it as a continuous and unedited version cannot be too strongly emphasized. The cameraman continued to explain the editing process as we viewed the film.

C.M.: There, see right here. See, we've taken that film . . . see his head is moving there, when he moves back it almost looks like a normal move; we're very lucky; you can see the splice line go across [the film viewer].

(The cameraman explains that usually you don't get that "lucky," [i.e., the guy usually moves more and it jumps].)

So what we've done, we've rolled that through and timed where that's going to occur, so . . . at 55 seconds in [the director will say] take B-roll, in which you'll see the B-roll come up and you'll see a wide shot of [reporter] standing there.

D.A.: Oh I see. In other words, at 55 seconds in that part you won't even see. . . .

C.M.: You won't even see it. All as you'll hear is his voice.

D.A.: I see.

C.M.: You should be able to hear just a . . . (he runs the film through the sound monitor) right there, where he says "variances," see off-camera reporter had said to him, "Say something about variances." Like I said, that should act as a pause, like he was collecting his thoughts. A lucky edit right there.

D.A.: You could use that?

C.M.: We could, yeah.

D.A.: But it is just better to do something else.

C.M.: And besides, it gives a little variety.

D.A.: How much B-roll will you run then?

C.M.: I think the first runs 15 seconds and the second runs 10 seconds, just long enough to get us over that physical jump there.

C.M.: (He explains again that the wide shot permits the viewer to see the
interviewee's lips moving, but not well enough to see that they are
not in sync. with the audio.)

D.A.: You generally try to use B-roll to get over the. . . .

C.M.: *Over the jump-cuts like that—always unless you don't have the B-roll
to cover it and you want to use the story, then you have to go to
the jump-cut. It's just a production technique.*

I then asked about time limitations, and if that didn't create some
problems with how the piece was edited. He continued:

C.M.: There is no problem; all as we have to do is put a head [i.e., establish
the identity of the speaker] and find out where we want to take
him out at, where we want to close.

The convenience of editing with narrative sequence in mind is
that it can always be achieved although the event may not have
occurred that way. If an interviewee states in his opening what
the interviewer regards as a good close, it is very easy to establish
the proper sequence or the order deemed most useful for presentational purposes. A story on atomic power plants illustrates this
process.

C.M.: We talked to a guy in an orange grove. We edit him twice; *the hard
thing about him is that [the reporter] wanted to take the last thing
he said—well, he said it earlier—but then again, in conforming to the
minute and forty some seconds that they're allowing these, it had to
run. He said, "Well, all we want as farmers is clean air, clean water,
and good land." [The reporter] wanted to use that 16 seconds so I
had to take that and put it in the last 16 seconds of film,* so that
meant I had to have B-roll going over the last 16 seconds. . . . I put
in a 20 second B-roll about 35 seconds in and brought in this last
16 seconds and had them turn and kind of walking off camera, and
then we cut to the [statement about "clean air" but God, I am
thankful now that I went ahead and shot all that wide stuff or we
wouldn't have anything to cover all these frigging edits we made.

It is apparent that these editing procedures are more than just
production techniques and that continuity is often gained at the

expense of how it actually happened, although these adjustments are not regarded as biased since the essential meaning is conveyed with more impact than the speaker intended: The statement, "All we want as farmers is clean air, clean water, and good land" is made as they walk off camera, when it actually occurred early in the interview.

Reporters and camera operators work in teams, but they often disagree about the best way to cover an event in order to tell a story about it. Putting film and a script together usually requires that one dominate, and the other follow. Usually, the camera operator is the one who follows the reporter's lead, but on occasion he may resist, especially if his partner's work creates a problem. Experienced reporters are aware of this delicate exchange. As one journalist put it: "The best way to make enemies here is to tell the photographer what to do, but the reporter is still responsible for the content."

"Rookie" reporters are often unaware of the power of the camera operator. While covering one story, a new reporter shouted orders to a veteran cameraman. The latter explained that his actions marked him as a rookie, and added that he would deal with him the same way he dealt with all those who "give me shit." In his words: "You fuck them by just letting them do what they want to do . . . there are lots of ways to make them look as shitty as they are."

From a cameraman's point of view, reporters who do not understand film create the most problems because in their rush to do their job, they ask their partner to violate common film sense. One cameraman explained that this is especially true of reporters who do not understand film and expect you to shoot five or ten seconds of this, and then pan to that, even though this violates the grammer of film (cf. Fang, 1968: 128). According to one cameraman, reporters "don't understand that the cameraman is also trying to do a good job," and that many of their requests are simply "poor aesthetically." One example is expecting cameramen to "patch" reporter's mistakes with silent film. As one film man put it, "All these guys think we can patch with B-roll all the time. They don't realize we've got to do it right." Diverse definitions of the situation were apparent in a story on sailing, where the reporter was sitting in a sailing simulator mounted on a trailer. The cameraman sought to give the impression that the trailered craft was afloat, until a wide angle shot would reveal the truth. After the first attempt failed, the following conversation occurred.

Rep: You got it?

C.M.: Yeah, it's okay. (He suggests getting more motion in the boat.)

Rep: I could rock it, I suppose.

C.M.: I mean, since you're talking about the simulator and you said you could simulate everything on the water, and it's still sitting here.

Rep: Okay, well I thought we'd do B-roll of that, but it doesn't matter. (The cameraman looks perturbed.) We can't do B-roll?

C.M.: Yeah, we could do B-roll.

Rep: Because I was afraid to do all of that [make the boat move] and manage the script because if this goddamn boom comes around and if we jib the son-of-a-bitch on this trailer, I'll be sitting out there somewhere] i.e., the water].

C.M.: Let's do it one more time.

The problem was that the reporter had a four-page script that was too long to memorize. However, in concentrating on sounding articulate, he had trouble getting enough motion for the cameraman. The following exchange occurred after the reporter had just blown his lines for the fourth time.

Rep: Oh [cameraman], forget it.

C.M.: God. Oh that was . . . you know, just before we started the people took off water skiing and the sailboat came by; you were moving it beautifully.

Rep: I just can't cut all that goddamn script and handling the boat . . . son-of-a-bitch.

C.M.: Oh, that was working out so good because we had nice movement in the background there and he was moving the boat and sailed it in front of me (laughs).

These comments suggest that those who work on news operate more with practical problems of their trade and equipment in mind, than with abstract formulations about social significance, objectivity, and the like. And these perspectives differ somewhat, depending on whether a newsworker is a news director, producer, assignment editor, camera operator, or reporter. Of course, the scene becomes even more complex at the network level where other separate tasks blend into the news brew, including electricians, grips, field producers, and film editors.

Summary

I noted earlier that time, scheduling, and practical problems do not permit careful analysis of various events. To the contrary, the aim is to tell a story about an event. Those assigned to work on news are responsible for finding something interesting about a happening and then telling about it in a story format. The news perspective is, then, the organizational answer to an awesome question: What daily events are important in this life? Even though the materials presented in this chapter illustrate that from the perspective of various newsworkers, what is important depends on the practical task at hand—and news cannot be understood without acknowledging this, the events that are transformed into news stories are not articulated in the same way. Newsworkers are the first to criticize those who accuse them of bias, partisanship, etc., by noting that outsiders are unaware of their routines and problems. Indeed, most critics do *not* understand their problems. By the same token, it would be unfair of me to criticize reporters for not sharing the assignment editor's view of news. I would be justly accused of not understanding their different problems and responsibilities even though we refer to both as newsworkers. In fact, their routine interests are quite diverse. But the same thing is true of the events covered on the nightly news; if it seems unfair to criticize news operations from a particular angle, then it is also unfair—in most cases—to summarily present an event from a predefined, and often barely informed, angle. Nevertheless, it occurs on a daily basis through the news perspective.

Chapter 4

THE NEWS PERSPECTIVE

Local News

The organization of newswork creates a number of practical problems for news personnel. How these are resolved may be viewed as the essentials of the evening news: scheduling, selecting, reporting, editing, writing, and presenting. These processes not only provide events to be treated as content for the newscast, but also contain the key ingredients to the news brew. From this perspective, any event is newsworthy if it is treated properly. During my research I have seen stories about defecating dogs, fifteen-cent robberies, treed cats, and pie-eating contests. However, the treatment process cannot be manifested in what is broadcast since that would, on occasion, undermine the public's belief in the organizational claims that "we don't make the news; we just report it." Thus, the good newscast is one which is put together along the lines noted throughout this book, but which bears no outward marks of this molding process. The news process shapes events into stories by distorting, however, and by emphasizing certain points over others. The impact of this work on local stories presented as news is my immediate focus. Several news items drawn from two cities illustrate how news practices are informed by the news perspective, and show that what is presented as news is a feature of a practical orientation. While these selections may not be representative of all news stories I have been involved with during the last several years, they do represent the perspective and procedures through which newsworkers see, and transform events into news reports.

The remainder of this chapter is divided into two sections. The first, called Issues and Answers, focuses on two interviews carried out in Phoenix, Arizona. These materials show how an interview is interpreted and edited to conform to a predefined story angle in order to support a foregone conclusion. The second part, called Newsworkers and Newsmakers: A Clash of Perspectives, highlights the news perspective on local stories by contrasting the way news-workers look at events with activists who seek to be newsworthy. The way the perspective of the former significantly alters the world view of the latter vis-à-vis the news process will be discussed.

Issues and Answers

Issues are problems that publics discuss. But what a problem is, and what the options for solving it are, do not emerge in a vacuum. News reports may prematurely foreclose the dimensions of some topic by trying to make sense out of it without careful examination, or by assuming that a particular issue is clear-cut. Two examples illustrate the way news procedures significantly alter what is said during an interview, and what is subsequently presented as the story. One interview concerns the aftermath of former President Nixon's pending decision to resign, and the impact it may have had on the country. I was the interviewee, and the interview was conducted by a reporter from a Phoenix station. The second interview, conducted by another local journalist, focuses on the shortage of freeways in Phoenix. The interviewee is an economics professor who specialized in transportation. The pre-camera discussion, and the filmed interchange was video-taped in each case. Noting the portions of these interviews that were used in the news stories, and the context in which they appeared, along with informal discussions with each of the reporters, provides further material for illustrating the news perspective.

A PRESIDENT RESIGNS

On August 7, 1974, two days before Richard Nixon resigned as President of the United States, a Phoenix TV reporter contacted the Department of Sociology at Arizona State University. He wanted to interview an "expert" about the impact of this resignation on the country. The late hour of the day, my availability, and a long-term research interest in news led to my involvement. Our off-camera discussion focused on what I would be asked.

Rep: One of the questions that I will ask you will be what do you think the fact that the stock market has sky-rocketed means.

D.A.: (laughter) What do you suppose it means?

Rep: And then finally I will probably ask you if all of this indecision represents a strain on the American public. And depending on your answers I may come up with other things.

D.A.: Okay, I'll try to put it in a certain perspective that is interesting to me and it may not be to you.

At this point the reporter knew that his story was about the impact of Nixon's decision on the national economic health and the strain on American psyches. But this was the preparation, or "warm up." When the camera rolled, I was asked:

Rep: Doctor, rumors have been flying all day long about the President resigning. There seems to be a lot of indecision. Does this have any effect on the American public?

D.A.: Well, that of course is very hard to say, across the board. I think that people are being flooded with a lot of information. I think the situation has been set up so that people are looking for a resolution to it, and I think a lot of people are trying very hard to resolve it, and presumably, when a resignation or an impeachment takes place, a crisis will have been averted, and a major problem will have been solved, and then we can go on from there. So I think a more interesting question would be, do people think it is going to be significant to the American people; that is, do the newsmen and congressmen think it is going to have a direct bearing on the American people. I am not at all certain that the American people have been extremely upset by it. But I think the more important point is that this is what spokesmen have felt.

Rep: You mentioned the word crisis. Is this in any way a crisis in the same
      sense that the assassination of President Kennedy was?

D.A.: Well, it is certainly unique in out history. I don't see it as that kind
       of crisis. I see it as an interesting way in which our judicial process
       is working itself out, and that if anything it is more of a statement
       to make to the American people, 'yes, indeed our processes are
       adequate, we do have good government; we don't have to worry
       about real corruption because it will be discovered.' *I think it would
       be a great disservice to the American people if they were led to be-
       lieve that all of the cankers are cut out and that from here on out
       everything is going to be fine. I think that would be a misstatement.*

It is apparent that the reporter's interest in the Nixon resignation
was different from mine. He was milking it for a story, or rather,
as we shall see below, as part of a bigger story. He focused on
specific points about a "crisis," for example, rather than trying
to understand how the idea of a crisis got started in the first place.
In short, he knew where the story was going, and needed the
materials to put it together. This is also evident in a brief excerpt
from our on-camera exchange about the meaning of an improving
stock market. My initial response, that a rising stock market could
mean a lot of different things, brought the following question.

Rep: Do you feel they're saying that if Nixon resigns, everything is going
      to be rosy?

D.A.: Well, again that's very difficult to say. I think it would be kind of
       unfair. I think a lot of things have probably come down to the
       point where people feel that, in terms of how the issues have been
       defined, that if he quits, a lot of problems will be resolved. And so
       to that extent, if they're reading it that way, you could say that
       [i.e., things will be rosy when Nixon steps down].

   This interview was then edited to fill in the more general story
presented by this station. This story turned on several angles. One
was the journalists' professionalism in not perpetuating rumors,
and instead, getting a direct and exclusive telephone interview
with Senator Goldwater. The anchorman opened the evening news
with the following statement.

A.M.: As if it has to be said, this is our top story: Arizona Senator Barry
Goldwater tells _____ news he feels the country could use new
leadership and he expects a presidential decision within 48 hours.
That news climaxes a day of rumor and confusion about the possibilities of President Nixon resigning. Newsman _____ is here with
us. He's been working on that story all day. What's the situation?

Rep: This day of rumor, and what has to be called national anxiety, nothing
less, began with early reports of a White House meeting this morning
between White House aide, General Alexander Haig, and Vice President Ford. Next there was speculation that congressional Republican
leaders would caucus and perhaps send a delegation to the White
House. At midday today two major newspapers, the Providence
Rhode Island *Review Journal* and the Phoenix *Gazette* hit the streets
with banner headlines proclaiming that according to exceptionally
dependable information, President Nixon would indeed resign today.
At one point in the afternoon an ABC newsman quoted Barry Goldwater as confirming the resignation and that added fuel to what was
becoming a bonfire. At noon today, _____ news began efforts to
get to the source, Senator Goldwater himself in order to clarify what
was becoming a major national confusion. At the conclusion of our
special coverage we have an exclusive, live telephone conversation
with Senator Goldwater.

After hearing Goldwater say that he felt the country could benefit
from new leadership and that he was certain Nixon would do what
was best for the country, listeners were reminded by the reporter
responsible for the exclusive telephone conversation:

> Apparently Senator Goldwater has not expressed those personal views
> to any other newsmen today. . . . Goldwater was irate today at mis-
> quotes on two television networks and he said that he regretted that
> neither those networks nor the [Phoenix] Gazette called him to ask
> him. Our news did.

Once the exclusive coverage had been established, the story moved
on to the local dimension other than a U.S. Senator. The anchorman made the transition, and prepared the viewer for excerpts
from "the man in the street."

A.M.: In the midst of all the chaos and uncertainty this afternoon, [our
reporter] went to the Park Shopping Center to find out what the
man in the street was thinking. He asked a random selection of
people if they thought President Nixon should resign or not.

After five anti-Nixon and three pro-Nixon men and women gave
their "man on the street" appraisals, the grim-faced anchorman
prepared the TV audience for the second theme in this story—
the persistence of American political institutions.

A.M.: There was a lot of worry today that the country, the government,
and the economy were all standing still because of this leadership
crisis, but there is also evidence that this is not true although what
our country is going through is painful, we will grow by it, we will
be better. Our news went to ASU to get the views of one sociologist.

The following excerpt of my statement was then presented without the important qualifying conclusion contained in the version
presented above.

D.A.: Well, it is certainly unique in our history. I don't see it as that kind
of a crisis. I see it as an interesting way in which our judicial process
is working itself out, and that if anything it is more of a statement
to the American people, 'Yes, indeed our processes are adequate,
we do have good government; we don't have to worry about real
corruption because it will be discovered.'

This ended the story, although the anchorman's transition to the
rest of the newscast emphasized its importance.

A.M.: On a day that hung on the verge of history, it is hard to believe that
anything else did make news, but there are other stories and we'll
report them next.

Several points must be emphasized. First, my interview was
part of a larger story that emphasized exclusive contacts with a
U.S. Senator, the ineptness of other media, including a local newspaper, the crisis our country was going through, and the general
impact on citizens and the economy. Answering such questions,
especially the last few, would demand thorough investigation and

a large amount of time. But the story was breaking fast, and it was being put together for the evening newscast, only hours away. All that was needed were statements from various people, including men on the street and an "expert" sociologist. My statements about the complexity of the issues, and even about the nature of the issues themselves, were completely ignored because they did not meet the requirements of the predefined story angles. Such distortion cannot be explained ideologically, or politically, without considering the nature of the news perspective and the practical problems that must be surmounted if news is to be presented in short, entertaining reports. Thus, as a sociologist, I was presented as saying what needed to be said to make the story hang together. And my complaints to the news director about the televised distorted messages were met with apologies and bewilderment—e.g., "What do you mean we perverted it?" From their perspective, I did not understand what news was all about.

TRAFFIC JAM PHOENIX

One of the common criticisms made of TV news in general, and especially of local news programs, is that they do not take enough time to investigate and thoroughly develop a story. This was part of the reason that the coverage about Nixon's resignation took the form it did. However, taking more time to develop a report does not guarantee that many of the problems discussed in this book will be resolved. *This is especially apparent with the news perspective: No matter how much time is devoted to an issue, if the options are predefined in order to make the story interesting or to comply with a reporter's persuasion about what is significant, then more time will make the report more detailed, but not necessarily more complete.* Rather, the details will be used as evidence that research has taken place, and as supporting materials for the news angle. This is apparent in an investigative report done by a local Phoenix station, "Traffic Jam Phoenix."

The thrust of the report, which ran for five nights during the evening newscast in October 1974, was that Phoenix needs more freeways. The reporter assigned to the project spent several weeks interviewing and talking with some two dozen officials, experts, and interested citizens about this issue. As with the Nixon resig-

nation story, interviewees were selected according to their presumed interest and/or expertise on the matter. A telephone conversation usually preceded an off-camera interview, which was
then followed by an on-camera interview. The latter was then
edited to fit with the overall story line. My study of this story
led me to video tape the complete on-camera interviews with two
experts on transportation and the controversy surrounding the
various arguments for and against such expanded roadways. In
addition, I video taped the complete off-camera interview with
one of these people, an economist, in order to show how the
on-camera discussion differed in content and presentational style
from the off-camera "warm-ups." These materials, along with
conversations with the reporter and cameraman, plus recordings
of the five-part special as it aired on the evening newscasts, permitted clarification of the dominant angle and the editing process.
That the reporter was already assured of the best way to resolve
the traffic problem in Phoenix is suggested by the following exchanges he had with the economics professor, a transportation
specialist.

Rep: How many miles of freeway do you think we need in Phoenix?

Prof: Well I don't know that. Because, you see, this is the purview of the
        engineer. So I don't really know how many miles we need. . . .
        I am an economist and we don't get into the actual matter of how
        many people use a given mile, etc. . . . So I can't answer that one.

Rep: In general, would you say we could use more freeways?

Prof: Yes, well certainly. I think there is a place that the through, freeway-
        type of highway has got to play . . . and it probably is one in which
        we can move people more efficiently on an intermediate basis than
        if we talk about fixed rail.

Rep: But you're going to need freeways anyway, aren't you, just to make
        rubber tire expressways go? In other words, if you want rubber
        tire mass transit, you need express lanes for them.

Prof: In the picture you're always going to have some moving by rubber
        tire vehicle in this kind of environment. . . . So there's not much
        question that there is a role for freeways. The crunch question is
        do you want to put your entire effort in that direction.

Rep: But what if you don't put any in that direction?

Prof: I would say that hopefully you could work this into your total plan that we were talking about on the phone.

The reporter's and economist's contrasting views on freeways were evident during a previous telephone conversation between them and during this phase of the warm-up discussion. The reporter believed freeways were immediately essential, while the economist was less convinced about their ultimate utility. Further discussion followed about the relevance of an improved bus system. The reporter felt more highways needed to be built before a bus system would work, whereas the economist saw it differently.

Rep: What about cross-town?

Prof: Now, you're talking in terms of freeways? Our greatest need in a relatively short term is cross-town bus service . . . but I can envision in the very near future with a very small investment by the public such things as cross-town bus service on a number of main streets. And do a considerable upgrading of the rubber tire transit system that we've got and make it more viable. *Without even a freeway*. Now in the longer picture you are going to probably have to have an increase in the streets, whether freeways are the thing to do or not. I am not sure about. . . .

Rep: I am just curious, you know, you expand your busing. Isn't that going to get bottled up in all of the garbage?

Prof: Well, yeah, but of course one of the answers to that, and again depending on your time frame, one of the things that we can do very easily is to have exclusive bus lanes during certain hours. This has worked in a number of places and is working very well. It is working right now in Washington, D.C. . . . Sure your buses are going to get bottled up if you expect them to go along in all of the regular traffic, but if you really put some effort behind the matter of urban transportation, exclusive bus lanes are a very easy thing to do.

The remaining minutes of the off-camera discussion focused on the nature of mass transportation in urban centers. The economist's suggestion that the word "mass" seems to "turn some people off" in the more individually oriented Southwest, led to the following comment:

Prof: Eventually we're going to have to give up part of this Southwest life
       style, in the sense that we're going to begin to move people in some-
       thing other than the private automobile.

This notion of "Southwest life style" played a big part in the way
the reporter approached the five special reports, but his version
of the transportation options differed substantially from the
economist's.

Upon completion of the pre-interview, the camera began to
roll, and many of the same issues were retreaded. The economist
emphasized that time frames needed to be set forth in order to
specify goals and practical ways to achieve them. When asked
about short-term solutions, he replied:

Prof: There's a lot of things and I think we are accomplishing some of these.
       . . . One of the first things we can do in the short term is begin to
       think in terms of the valley, an areawide transportation rather than
       thinking in terms of individual cities. . . . We've made some progress
       there. Some of the physical sorts of things such as changing on-
       street parking to off-street parking, perhaps having exclusive bus
       lanes during certain hours, certain devices the traffic engineers come
       up with to expedite and move traffic. . . . A number of those things
       can be done with very little investment.

He then emphasized that the current freeway system could be
more efficiently used.

Prof: We have a tremendous investment already made in our freeway system
       that exists; we do not use it very much for buses, for express serv-
       ices, and that investment is already there, particularly when you
       compare it to the tremendous investment of fixed rail or people
       mover system.

The reporter noted that the freeway system does not really go
anywhere where people want to go. The interviewee explained
that our freeways were built to move people around Phoenix and
not through it. The reporter's query, "Do we need more freeways?" was answered as follows.

Prof: Oh, I think it has a place to play, certainly. As we begin to look down
       the line . . . we have to have some freeways to move some of this

through traffic around town, some sort of an outer-belt system or something of that nature. . . . And some sort of an expedited system to move cars within our cities.

The interviewee was also convinced that a fixed-rail type of transit is probably not feasible since the current densities are not adequate to support such a system. However, he made the point very clearly that it was hard to predict just how fast the area would grow in the future.

Prof: It is hard to put a date, because . . . we're making an estimate about how Phoenix is going to grow, and we know that these growth patterns have varied tremendously. Look at 1950, 1940, and if you had to project 1970, gee, it presents a problem.

But he was convinced that transportation difficulties would eventually lead to changes in the southwestern life style.

Prof: We're going to have to have some changes and we're not going to be able to maintain the present type of life style and solve our transportation problems.

The interviewee then reiterated his view that the short-term changes should involve improving the bus system and making it go where people want to go, and not just into and out of downtown. This ended the filmed interview.

The interview materials were edited to fit the central theme of the five-part series: that Phoenix desperately needed a freeway system. Only three brief comments by the economist were used in the entire series. The first excerpt was the interviewee's lack of enthusiasm for fixed rail and other people-mover systems. This position was consistent with the reporter's thrust that freeways would be better. After noting the difficulties that other cities have had with most transit, the reporter rhetorically asked, "Would such systems work in Phoenix?" The economist responded:

There is a great tendency on the part of America to fall in live with hardware, with shiny things and new things. They're feasible here if we get up to a certain destiny. It would be my judgment that probably the only place they would perhaps be used would be up and down

North Central and in the government corridor, and even then not until
we hit densities like 10,000 people in the peak hour and we're only
about half that . . . at the present time.

Selections from other interviews were then used to show the
enormous cost of a fixed rail, or related type of system. After
dismissing mass transit as a workable alternate, the reporter questioned the merit of an expanded bus system.

In Phoenix we have fewer than 100 [buses]. Ridership is up 23% this
year, but still only about ½ of 1% of our traveling public use buses
daily. City hall critics say there are not enough buses, they're not on
time, and they don't go where people want to go.

An excerpt from a "city hall critic" noted that many elderly
people drive automobiles who should not be driving, and that if
there was a bus system that ran on time, most of them would be
happy to give up their cars. Another cut from the economist was
then used.

Everything goes into and comes out of downtown. No cross-town
service, for instance, not a hatch-system in which you go across town.
And so it is rather difficult for some people to utilize it. We've got to
rethink our bus system not only in terms of buses, but where the buses
go and they need to go where the people need to go . . . right now, unfortunately, there is too little of this.

The final section of the interview that was used concerned the
more efficient use that could be made of current transportation
modes. "We have a tremendous investment already made in our
freeway system that exists; we do not use it very much for buses
. . . for express services."

This was followed by the reporter's appraisal of these short-
term solutions. While acknowledging that improved bus service
could contribute to a total transportation plan, the reporter stated
it was not enough in the long run. Despite the economist's warn-
ings about projecting population growth, and noting how uncertain such changes could be, the reporter extrapolated current
trends to bolster the story line that increases demand more roads,
including freeways.

The population of automobile-oriented Phoenix today is 750,000. By 1985 we'll pass the one million mark with a metro population of two million. Suburban Glendale had 36,000 people in 1970; today that's up to 70,000. You get the picture. . . . Today there are about 56,000 residents in Paradise Valley; there will be 88,000 by 1980. That's the type of growth that could create an awesome traffic crunch.

Such projected growth patterns seemingly call for drastic action to avert a rapidly approaching catastrophe. A portion of an interview with the city traffic engineer made this conclusion clear:

Rep: Someday, you're going to run out of these short-term cures, aren't you? What then?

Eng: Sure, we're going to run out of them, and we need a better street system, and frankly, as traffic engineer of this city, I must say that we need a freeway system.

Rep: Does that mean an east-west, cross-town system?

Eng: Sure we need an east-west cross-town freeway, and we need some north-south freeways.

Another section of the report emphasized the authoritative consensus about the need for freeways.

Rep: The mayor, city and state transportation experts all say we need freeways, but anti-freeway voices remain strong, while our numbers grow. What will break the ice and get transportation planning in high gear again? We'll examine that tomorrow in the last of our special series, "Traffic Jam Phoenix."

The last report stressed the theme which ran throughout the series: that freeways were the only viable means to maintain a Western life style.

Rep: Here's where we stand today: The fewest number of freeway miles of any major U.S. city; an inadequate city bus system that has yet to convince people they should ride rather than drive; a major street system that daily grows more incapable of handling our rush-hour traffic; the fastest-growing population of any major urban area in the country; a Western life style that realistically commits us to a long-term marriage to our automobiles.

Apparently, the reporter's earlier point that bus riders increased by twenty-three percent the previous year did not detract from the contention that people were not riding the bus more. Equating more freeways with solving the traffic crunch was again evident in the investigator's closing remarks:

Rep: In solving "Traffic Jam Phoenix," planners probably can convince people of the need for a large-scale, cross-town bus system, and better streets. That's part of the answer, but it's not enough. Our research tells us that as soon as possible we will have to make a very tough choice. The choice is this: Either add an expanded freeway system to our transportation formula or scrap the idea of more freeways. Freeways might preserve much of our spread-out life style and provide corridors for high-speed express buses. Without freeways, we'll probably have to abandon that so-called Western life style and build a high-density city that makes an expensive rapid transit system economically feasible. There are social and aesthetic disadvantages to freeways. The same can be said about high-density living. Now is the time to make a decision if we are going to solve "Traffic Jam Phoenix."

Several points must be made about the interview with the economist and the way it was subsequently edited to fit into the five-part series. First, the reporter was convinced from the outset that there was a traffic problem and that freeways were the best solution to it. The implications of expanded freeways for increased air pollution, greater reliance on automobiles, and the disadvantages to those citizens who do not drive were largely irrelevant. Second, no effort was made to compare the efficacy of freeways in Phoenix with other freeway cities, such as Los Angeles, in order to discover, for example, whether or not freeways provide viable solutions to transportation problems, or whether, as some planners have suggested, freeways become clogged in direct proportion to their availability. Third, the angle of maintaining our Western life style was used as the highest priority, which is evident from the bizarre reasoning that the alternative to a freeway city was high-density living. Moreover, it will be recalled that the economist who was interviewed made it very clear that ultimately continuing suburban sprawl and solving some transportation problems were largely contradictions, and that some of the convenience and freedom of driving our cars wherever and whenever we choose would probably have to be given up. Indeed, very few of the professor's comments were incorporated in the reports because he was used as a resource for the journalist to draw on. This leads to a related point: The reporter's "research" consisted of obtaining evidence to tell the story the way he saw it and to develop his very limited perspective on the transportation issue and its alternatives.

These points have direct bearing on the question of objectivity raised earlier in this work. Although a more detailed discussion of this important topic will follow in Chapter 7, it is appropriate to highlight the relevance of these materials for some common journalistic notions of objectivity. One of the most common approaches to avoid bias in journalism is to not only tell both sides of a story, but also to directly quote people. In this way, distortion is partially avoided, and the person speaks for himself. The final report, with the possible exception of the reporter's analysis, is then said to consist of the facts. That is, this is how it is with transportation, freeways, and the life style in Phoenix, and this is the proof of it. As Tuchman (1972) and others have pointed out, this practical approach to objectivity leaves many problems unsolved, including the selection and editing process. In the cases noted above, however, there are even more severe problems involving the definition of the issue and the artful use of people as advocates, scholars—and perhaps shills—to tell it the way it seems to be within the confines of accepted news frames.

Equally important was the way that giving both sides of the issue did not detract from the reporter's position. Being "fair" did not resolve the most systematic bias in this story. The news perspective led the reporter to reduce a very complex issue into a simple problem: Are we or are we not going to have more freeways? The angle of maintaining a Western life style showed how important an affirmative answer was. This conclusion was reiterated in a station editorial one week after the last of the special reports was aired. According to this opinion,

> We need to build more freeways as part of an overall transportation plan. With our low-density, spread-out Western life style, we simply cannot afford the price of fancy rail-based mass transit in Phoenix.

What the citizens of this southwestern community could afford, according to this editorial, were a better bus service and "more freeways."

Viewers of this newscast were told a story about freeways, the Western life style, and how they were related. And this was done over a period of several weeks and not in a few hours, as is true of most news reports. Nevertheless, the power of the news perspective made angles appear as facts rather than a feature of reporting, editing, and presenting procedures.

The most crucial aspect of the news perspective is that it is not identified as such by newsworkers who routinely employ it to give us the day's significant events, issues, and, in this case, possible solutions. This is the first thing that must be recognized: *News is the product of an organized process which entails a practical way of looking at events in order to tie them together, make simple and direct statements about their relationship, and do this in an entertaining way.* The way most stories are presented, however, obfuscates these procedures, and more often than not, what we see makes sense; without very careful reflection, the messages seem to follow logically from the evidence.

The next section examines what the news perspective looks like to those outside the news scene. Examining the way two activists conceive of news, and understanding how stories are defined, selected, and presented, illustrates how finished news stories are replete with practical compromises.

Newsworkers and Newsmakers: A Clash
of Perspectives

The news value of an event is *usually* subject to disagreement, but is *always* contingent on the interests and needs of news personnel. Most news agents would agree that major events such as an assassination or declaration of war deserve to be reported. Such developments are commonsensically important to a lot of people; the news people are primarily conveying information in these cases. But even these are not so clear cut. For example, I heard one assignment editor in a network owned and operated station argue that Kissinger's famous "peace is at hand" speech about the Vietnam war in September 1972 did not deserve the extensive coverage it received. It was just another talking head, and very little of substance was conveyed. After all, he explained, the war has not ended, and it may be part of Nixon's strategy to insure reelection. Nevertheless, the speech received extensive play, even though this journalist's suspicions were borne out as the war dragged on until Nixon took credit for ending it. Despite these disagreements over what is newsworthy, newsworkers agree in word and deed that they know what news is, and that this may vary with a situation and with day-to-day scheduling needs. But it is their practical interests which prevail even though persons outside the news scene may disagree. Indeed, the taken-for-granted —and often explicated—pronouncement that the world has been adequately combed for the strongest news fiber to weave a significant account of the day is another central feature of the news perspective: News is what news people say it is. This claim is seldom articulated, since part of the modus operandi of news personnel is that the events occur "out there," and they simply report them. To argue that they make, or arbitrarily select, news would be contrary to their epistemological stance, an implicit theory of knowledge built on practical procedures to resolve organizational demands.

The news perspective has great implications for what is presented to viewers. Not only are stories selected for specific reasons, but the subsequent treatment by newsworkers significantly alters "what happened." Most striking, perhaps, is the transformation which occurs in everyday life when those outside regularly used news channels seek to be included in news reports. When the day's news events are selected and constituted by the news perspective, then those wanting access to this crucial medium must adjust to the perspective. In short, I am suggesting that the news scene has developed, and continues to perpetuate, a self-fulfilling prophecy: Events to be included must be compatible with a perspective which scans the world for significance (cf. Elliott, 1972). *This means that the news perspective, which began as a practical way to separate one event from another, and then make plausible statements about it within a very confined time, has now come to set the criteria for importance.* Two examples of the perceived importance of news coverage, and the significance of playing to the perspective of newsworkers, follow. Examining the strategies to be filmed and presented as significant illustrates the power of the news perspective in shaping activities intended to be news.

The practicalities of the news process become clearer when contrasted with the points of view of newsmakers who seek news coverage. One political activist was encountered when he came to Channel B to talk about news coverage of a forthcoming event. A taped interview, and subsequent follow-up on the coverage of that event, provided a backstage glimpse at media politics. Another activist, a friend and member of a minority group organization, kept me informed of ongoing plans to stage a demonstration to obtain media coverage of a congressional investigation about discriminatory acts by immigration officials at an international crossing. Their perspective on news will be illustrated, and briefly contrasted with that of newsworkers, in regard to: defining and recognizing news, selecting stories, and covering and presenting stories. The common concerns of both will clarify what the newsmakers sought to promote and get across through strategies to obtain news coverage, as well as illustrate how newsworkers evaluated their efforts as "tactics" and actually covered the stories.

DEFINING AND RECOGNIZING NEWS

The definition of news is always pragmatic. Chapter 3 showed that what is practical cannot be divorced from the content in which an event is to have significance. We have seen that scheduling and commercial constraints, as well as presentational forms and entertainment motifs, lead newsworkers to look for news in certain places at certain times. This organizational and professional point of view is not shared by those who perceive news coverage more strategically. One political activist complained that Channel B did not cover a press conference for the first Chicano woman to run for national office. His query, "Don't you think that's worth something?" was balanced by his understanding of news value a few moments later when he added, "The only time they [TV stations] show up is if there is a demonstration or something." From this perspective news is part of a larger battle to receive recognition and be treated as a legitimate voice—as legitimate as the mayor and superintendent of schools when they look the camera in the eye and lie.

Encountering obstacles to obtain news coverage leaves two options: (1) be passive and hope that the camera lens will some-day illuminate your problems, or (2) use strategy to obtain news coverage. Two activists chose the second option. One informant explained what was involved in the decision to have a demonstration to draw attention to upcoming congressional hearings on the abuse of power by immigration officials.

> The chair wanted to know if we should have a demonstration at all or rather the hearings would generate their own publicity. . . . A reporter on one of the newspapers [who] was also a victim of abuse [at the border] mentioned that it would be very hard to get more than just normal publicity out of this thing . . . if something dramatic wasn't done because the news media doesn't normally pay attention to the normal happenings; someone determines what's news and most of the time your stuff will end up in the wastebasket and there's just no way of getting it across. . . . The news desk or manager have [sic] very concrete concepts of what news is and this does not include the minority community. They're not news unless they're opposed to the structure, and then they're news. So, then we decided to take a consensus as to whether to stage this thing [i.e., the demonstration].

After making it clear to the committee that he felt "demonstrations were a stupid way of carrying out any meaningful action," my informant added,

> I would have to be for it because we didn't control the mass media and there was no other way of getting the type of attention this thing deserved unless there was some type of demonstration. . . . At the meeting there was a general feeling expressed of complete unhappiness with the presentation of the mass media. It was brought up continually that the only media coverage we get is when we are in a bad light [he cites several examples, including a Chicano border guard charged with illegally selling immigration papers]. The general tenor of the meeting was that the mass media is there only when there is something that is objectionable.

Another activist, who was involved in focusing public attention on police efforts to criminalize hitchhiking was frustrated when the Sheriff's Department established an identical policy. He also defined news in practical terms.

With the Chief of Police we [could] go before the City Council; with the Sheriff we couldn't go before the County Board of Supervisors because the Sheriff is an elected official and the Chief of Police is appointed and is responsible to the City Council; so with the Sheriff, all we could do is go to [him] and he gave me a rap of about 45 minutes [that their hitchhiking policy is a good thing] *so there was nothing we could do except put out a [news] release.* So I called up the station [Channel B] and talked to [reporter].

The press release was viewed as a tactic in obtaining news coverage to combat the Sheriff's efforts. This strategy was not developed in a social vacuum but was informed by a partial understanding of the practical problems of newswork—namely, if the story is good, reporters may cover it, but the source must be reliable. This same activist explained how his relationship to newsmen was built on this understanding.

We always follow up on the [tips] and a lot of the things that we do happen to be newsworthy . . . like trying to stop the appointment of the Police Chief. That made headlines for about three days.

Both activists speak to the utility of news. On the one hand, news personnel are regarded as being uninterested in their problems, while on the other hand, news is an answer to these problems. The central thrust, however, is that news is useful. This definition is clearly different from the perspective of newsworkers, but the two purposes are occasionally brought into line through newsworthy events.

SELECTING STORIES

What is presented as news is contingent on what is done to produce a newscast. While institutionalized sources provide the events-to-be-presented-as-news, and their exclusion from these sources led the activists to scheme for TV coverage, some events will be selected on the basis of scheduling needs, capacity and time to get to an event and film it, and entertainment value. Indeed, the format and the need to have a certain number of stories forces the assignment editor to come up with news even during a slow day. Just as journalists present stories for practical and individual gain—recall the story about the racket-ball baron in Chapter 3— the political activists I studied were interested in news for reasons other than holding forth objective information.

Newsmakers aimed to have their interests presented as news. They understood, however, that their activities were unlikely to be included in the institutional news sources. This prompted a concern for playing to the newsworker's criteria of news in order to attract their attention, but, most importantly, letting them know about the event in terms that would be practical and understandable. One essential aspect of their plans to obtain news coverage was knowledge of who newsmen were, and which ones would be interested in their type of story. They would never ask someone for coverage "to help us out" because this would be met with a flat denial as compromising the integrity of newswork. Their option was to go directly to the assignment editor or a friendly reporter with a tip. One activist explained how he maintained relationships with the media:

> It just works like I told you. You give tips to people and you do it so it's pretty fair, like you'll give a tip to [reporter at Channel A] one time, and the next time I'll give it to [reporter at Channel B] or to [editor]; another time I will give it to [various reporters at the local newspapers]. *But the point is that you give somebody an exclusive, or a jump on the story, and they appreciate that.*

This activist systematically established ties with the various news media and would generally contact all of them to get his message out. He understood their procedures.

> Generally, I usually handle the releases; I'll take a release and go down and see the person; I don't mail them; I go personally and hand it to them and tell them what's happening and so on, give them the names of people to call that are connected with the issue, including the opposition . . . and radio stations I will just call up.

This knowledge of procedure gives him an advantage over newsworkers who must *derive* their stories from uninteresting assignments; the activist *provides* newsworthy stories.

Tips help reporters and thereby insure more coverage for the relevant event. This requires more detailed understanding about how media differ in format, organization, and the size of news staffs. The importance of giving the stations a package that fits their schedule is suggested by the following exchange (using fictitious call letters):

Activist: I find I no longer have to formulate the release as such and type it up. I just do it in my head and make the one-minute release or whatever I know that particular station takes. Some will take two minutes; CABD usually takes two minutes; DEAC usually wants it kept down to half a minute or forty-five seconds, and you learn those sorts of things.

D.A.: What about Channel B?

Activity: Well, Channel B, you can give a fairly large release to because they've got a large enough staff to work up a story and they can edit, add to it, they can investigate it, whereas radio stations like BAC or ACB or CAB can't do that; they only have two-man staffs and at any one time they usually have only one man there and some of them have mobile units; BAC has one mobile unit; CAB has one mobile unit, but ACB doesn't; CABD doesn't. So, you know, you have to be careful. The television stations and newspapers you don't have to hassle because they have the staff to go into it.

News success for this activist hinged on an awareness of the organizational and scheduling priorities and limitations. To give a news operation a story it cannot possibly cover, even if it wants to, is a waste of everyone's time. Conversely, to provide the news outlets with an interesting and manageable story is to be one step closer to the microphone or camera—e.g., challenging the appointment of the police chief "made headlines for about three days."

A similar bargain was struck at Channel B when a trusted reporter was leaked information by a federal official who claimed that his superiors were succumbing to political pressure to withhold indictments against corrupt immigration officials. The reporter began an investigative report and threatened to publicize the holdup. The superiors, fearing public reprisal, began to do their jobs and handed down the indictments a short time later. In this way, a news leak provided a conscientious civil servant with leverage needed to force others to fulfill their responsibility, but it also provided a reporter with more material for an award-winning investigative report.

We have seen that non-newsmen who seek to use the news must provide information compatible with the news interests. However, getting a story across does not mean that it will be selected, especially if the reporter is not interested. Reporters will usually cover their assignments even if they do not think they are newsworthy; otherwise they may be fired. The reporter has more leeway when dealing directly with the tipster. For one thing, he cannot get in trouble for refusing to pursue a "questionable lead," and, for another, he may have to invest hours of his own time. For these reasons, many reporters would rather avoid the inconvenience than take a chance, although these decisions are always colored by the story and how much confidence they place in their information source.

The reporter's perspective and interest play an important part in assessing the motivation of the tipster. In the case of the federal official noted above, the reporter was already interested in the story, and he was aware of the official's motives, even if they were largely irrelevant to him. If the *story* is not relevant to the newsman, the promoter's purpose may be called into question—e.g., "they just want publicity." This happened when a political activist attempted to stage a demonstration to draw media attention. Channel B never showed the demonstration on either of its newscasts even though a cameraman was on the scene. I asked a reporter why the story had not been shown.

> Everybody knew they were going to have a protest. . . . Yeah, everybody has a little demonstration . . . everybody wants to get on TV, and you know, they know they can do it—but we just don't do that anymore.

The irony was drawn: My informant's understanding of what would be newsworthy was not similarly held by newsmen. The primary reason was that "everybody wants to get on TV," and demonstrations had become so commonplace over the years that they were now suspected of being staged for publicity. The problem was that newsworkers had come to despise the scenario that was seen by the activists as strategically necessary for publicity.

COVERING AND PRESENTING STORIES

News is not an object, but is defined, selected, covered and presented for specifiable purposes. We have seen that conflicting claims about news judgment, fairness, and the selection of stories turn on different uses of news. This is also true of different perspectives on how events-treated-as-news should be covered and presented.

Groups outside the news organization are also interested in how accurately their stories are covered and presented. While they want publicity, they are also aware that the story must be newsworthy to newsworkers. This means that the event they promote should be compatible with one of the common news angles referred to earlier.

Members of a political organization felt that a strategy—a demonstration—was essential to attract media attention to the congressional hearings about the conduct of immigration officials. One of the silent promoters was a congressman who sought to cure his failing image among his constituents with a good dose of news. As an informant explained, "I think he is afraid there won't be adequate coverage and no purpose will have been served for him."

This lawmaker was not alone in his interest in a demonstration, although there was some disagreement about the specific aims. One activist described a meeting where plans had been discussed.

> So the main problem was to determine how to come about with a unified coalition stand in order to be able to verbalize the specific ends or goals of this particular meeting. What it was, in other words, we're going to get out of it, and that's where the meeting began to break down because the more radical elements wanted to use the meeting or the hearings as a means of blowing steam off about the entire system, totally diffused and incoherent; you know, they were striking at state government, federal government, all the realm of problems that are faced by minorities, which is kind of stupid.

This man worried lest their demonstration "turn people off" and work against the avowed goal of using the news media to arouse public support. He then described what he would like to see happen.

I would like to see similar to what had been carried on in the South where they had the representation from the established Negroes, you know, the blacks in suits and ties, middle-class establishment, right along with the youth, right along with all levels of society . . . a broad-based demonstration that is populated by all levels of people, not only the young radicals, bearded, hippy, which is so stigmatized in our community . . . as soon as they see that they're turned off.

The decision was made at the next meeting to have the demonstration.

It is one thing to get media coverage but it is another matter to get the kind of coverage and presentation that is desired. However, of the two, coverage is easier to engineer than presentation. The latter is more difficult to influence since the news operations have their purposes, too, and these may not be shared by the people promoting an event's coverage. The relevance of these different intentions can be seen with a political activist's endeavors to raise questions about the anti-hitchhiking policy. His plan appeared to backfire when the local newspapers presented what he described as "vicious coverage."

The way the *Gazette* handled this was they put a picture of a girl hitchhiking and they said Mary will no longer have to comply with the police hitchhiking program, the city manager rules. . . . And they put under that a very gory story telling about all kinds of ugly things that happened to girls and such—it was very sexist—and right under that they put the city manager's ruling . . . and starting with the first paragraph they went on how we went before the City Council and sought to stop the hitchhiking program and it just made us like we were dirty bastards, you . . . it just was vicious . . . the juxtaposition of the stories and that manner in which it was done.

The story was "vicious" because it was told from an angle unfavorable to the activist. Another example of the newsworker's angle guiding the interpretation of the newsmaker's facts is the news coverage of a trial for resisting the draft. The newsmaker explained.

There were some things that I wanted to bring up. . . . I was so closely tied in with the issue, that I think some things are important . . . I

wanted to develop the fact [that] here I was resisting because I felt
that I was already serving society by . . . trying to change injustices
[resisting against] destroying property and destroying people [but]
the media just didn't think that was good enough, interesting, or
whatever and they focused more on the actual trial.

The final example of the different interests of news organizations and those involved in news stories is the coverage of the
demonstration and congressional hearings. The demonstration
received very little coverage, while the hearings were presented
throughout the news spectrum. The two newspapers ran front-
page articles, and both television stations presented film reports
on several newscasts. However, the coverage was not exactly what
the activists had in mind. Channel B's report nicely illustrates the
different purposes of the promoters and one newsman. Whereas
the various factions of the coalition desired to utilize the demonstration and hearings for their purposes, and a congressman sought
to continue his political career through media exposure, one of
Channel B's reporters was hard at work on an investigative report
delving into another aspect of the border situation. He sought to
utilize the border hearings as a "lead" into his own report on the
involvement of immigration officials in permitting aliens to enter
the country illegally. This interest influenced the coverage of the
congressional hearings. The reporter instructed the cameraman
who covered the hearings to get enough silent film to cover the
opening of his own border series which began several days later.
The reporter's introduction to what became an award-winning
investigative report suggests an interest unshared by the other
players in this media game.

A congressional subcommittee investigating alleged abuses of persons
crossing the international border . . . held hearings here. . . . The subcommittee received a great deal of attention from the news media,
yet this committee and others have overlooked other pestering more
serious problems at the border. For example, the sale of border crossing documents to Mexican aliens and apparent corruption in the U.S.
Immigration Service.

The reporter's purpose was different from that of those seeking
to benefit from publicity on the hearings. He used the event to

promote his report by treating the hearings as evidence of continual oversights regarding border corruption, while the political organization was bent on using the hearings to document continued discrimination. News was useful to each, although the journalist was able to exercise a gatekeeping option not available to the activist. The final story would have been different if the latter's interest had been more in keeping with the reporter's intent. This does not mean that there was a winner, nor does it mean that there was a battle between the two media agents. Both promoters were satisfied with their work, but the journalist seemed more suspicious of attempts to use the news by outsiders, while the activist remained convinced that some strategy was useful when entering the news scene. Both had practical reasons for involvement with news stories, but the newsmakers were convinced that their events must meet the criteria they believed guided news agents as they selected and then reported events. This means that the packaging or presentation of everyday life must remain oriented to the kind of wrappings preferred by news judgments. Moreover, the presentational forms may be worn out with use, as was the demonstration tactic; it had been very successful during the civil rights days and received a lot of media attention. But now that civil rights was no longer "big news"—and nothing can remain news for long—the activists' strategy communicated a contrivance rather than a genuine concern. And it was contrived! However, the contrivance was believed essential to catch the camera's eye since the world the activists knew was not otherwise newsworthy.

Summary

The influence of practical organizational concerns on the way newsworkers approach stories was shown with interview materials from two stories. The second part of this chapter was intended to illustrate how various groups have an interest in news, although the way newsworkers defined, selected, and presented events-as-news is not well understood by those outside the news scene. This suggests that events are newsworthy for practical reasons and not for their objective character.

All of these materials point to the unique way news agents approach events and problems. The power of the angle in fitting circumstances to prior conclusions, beliefs, and practices, permits complex questions to be encapsulated, but loses something in the process.

The relationship between news purposes and news reports is further demonstrated in the coverage of the National Political Conventions, the subject of Chapter 5.

Chapter 5

LOCAL AND NATIONAL NEWS

The Political Conventions

News reports reflect the procedures that change events into stories. I have shown how this operates at the local level. The purposes of news personnel at the stations discussed in Chapters 3 and 4 informed both the selection and the presentation of news events. Network reports also show the imprint of practical reasoning, although there are important differences from local operations. Seldom do network and local news crews encounter the same event, and it is even more rare—with the exception of natural catastrophes—for them to deal with the event in the same way. The similarities and differences between the two media become even sharper when one event is viewed from the perspective of each. To analyze these similarities and differences, I attended both National Political Conventions in 1972.

National stories are not substantively different from local stories. They do differ in presentational form and their presentational medium: network newscasts. Epstein (1973) shows that most of the network domestic news comes from five cities, including Washington, D.C. News from these cities is "nationalized" by its presentation as having national significance because it often involves political decisions and personalities which may affect lives throughout the country. However, the majority of news from the other cities can be covered as local news in local stations. But the networks may cover the same events, claiming that they either represent national trends or are examples of some larger issue, such as racial problems, busing controversies, alienation, and the like. One way of nationalizing a local story is to couch it in such broader issues, while playing down local particulars which would be unfamiliar to viewers thousands of miles away—for example, not including street names or other geographical markers. It is not uncommon for a network affiliate to provide film of an event to a network which is likely to assign one of its own people to write the story in the appropriate manner.

One of the major differences between national and local stories, then, is that the former appear on network newscasts, while the latter do not. Newsworkers understand this. They know, for example, that a local story can be picked up by a network—a contingency they regard as favorable recognition for the reporter and cameraman involved, and which is often seen as a first step to a network career.

Another important difference is the news sources available to local and network operations. As noted previously, network news has correspondents throughout the world and an immensely bigger budget than the local crews. And the networks tend to rely more on wireservice reports along with their reporters, and other sources, in the nation's capital. The major factor is money and personnel. Further, local operations know that some stories will more than likely be covered by the networks, since the latter have more resources. This is why a large forest fire in Los Angeles will seldom be covered by a reporter from San Francisco; the latter's assignment editor knows that he can tape it from the network feed.

Access, resources, and a national audience are important ingredients of national stories, but the way such stories are presented is even more distinctive. National stories are about events reported as significant for people not immediately affected by the events, which is why fluctuations in the stock market are more important than a small-town fire which kills three people.

The national news story facilitates informing the audience about an event by placing it in some kind of perspective. The effort to make sense out of an event and thereby fully appreciate its significance also enables a reporter to plan his coverage. This presentational orientation encourages journalists to emphasize the context or broader implications of an event at the expanse of the specifics; the latter often become evidence of the context which was independently derived. Paul Weaver (1972) refers to this practice as the use of *themes* which link one report to another over a period of days. Weaver and his associates (Ferguson, 1972) found that television coverage of some presidential candidates during the 1972 campaign was influenced by definitions carried over from one story to another.

> *Edmund Muskie.* Television news coverage of Senator Edmund Muskie was overwhelmingly dominated by a single theme—that of the 'frontrunner.' . . . Muskie attempted to portray himself as the candidate of trust and of hope, the enemy of division, the unifier of his party and his country. But the newsmen interpreted this stance largely as a mere tactic of the frontrunner who employs only empty rhetoric because he does not wish to risk losing any of his support by taking clearcut stands.

> *George McGovern.* As Senator Muskie's principal opponent in New Hampshire, George McGovern was identified by the network news programs as the 'underdog' in that state's primary election. . . . Other important themes which recurred in the reporting of McGovern's campaign [were] the constituency . . . the appeal to the 'alienated' voter [and the] theme of the 'two Georges' of 'the new populism' was used to explain the growing strength McGovern showed among blue collar workers in Wisconsin and in some later primaries.

> *George Wallace.* Television news . . . never treated George Wallace as a serious contender for the Democratic nomination. . . . The focus on most coverage . . . became the Wallace phenomenon rather than the Wallace candidacy, and the dominant themes dealt with the Alabama governor's constituency . . . a populist . . . *the* anti-busing candidate [italics in original].

> *Hubert Humphrey.* [His] personality provided the important theme of his television coverage. The news stories frequently emphasized Humphrey's remarkable exuberance and his indefatigable energy as a cam-

paigner—*despite his 60 years* . . . the 'happy warrior' . . . the 'old war-horse' . . . 'the politician of the past' was also evident in the treatment given to Hubert Humphrey's constituency [italics in original].

The use of themes to present trends further distinguishes national from local stories: many of the trends have national significance, but they cannot usually be fully explored in the few minutes available for each newscast. In the proper context, however, a single theme can be taken as evidence of these trends. This strategy can also draw on angles for a specific story. For example, the theme of "confident frontrunner" may be supported by different angles such as he "is not making many public appearances," "feels no pressure to discuss the issues," and the like. An angle may also be used independently of a theme, or it may be used as an example of a more encompassing theme. Which strategy is selected will depend on whether the event is presented as a continuing story or as an isolated event.

The upshot is that any event may be newsworthy if it can be told in the right way. This is why it is common for journalists to agree on the *facts* but disagree on the *story*. I have heard local reporters complain that the network "boys" really "screw up" many of the reports which originate with the affiliates. The network people must make a national story out of a local happening, and this entails a unique perspective since, in the final analysis, all events are local: The events occur in a particular time and place, but journalistic analysis can diminish geographical and temporal parameters.

These brief comments about news are intended to clarify the news perspective. The most distinctive feature of this outlook is that events are seldom examined in their own right, but are understood and pursued within the practical boundaries of organizational and presentational concerns. This perspective encourages journalists to look at events in order to tell a story about them rather than to convey them so the audience understands them. Our task here is to show how the 1972 National Political Conventions were presented along similar lines.

Political Conventions as News Events

According to NBC's anchorman, John Chancellor, network coverage of National Political Conventions gives the voter a chance to be an eyewitness to a very important democratic process. But what the viewers witness is filtered through news organizations. Contrasting the orientation and coverage by network and local news personnel illuminates the way differing national and local stories are constructed from the same event.

More than 7,000 news personnel from all over the world were involved with each convention in 1972. Only about twenty-five percent were camera operators or reporters. The remainder were support personnel such as technicians, who transformed the convention complex into a television studio. This required extensive adjustments in lighting, air-conditioning (to combat the heat resulting from increased "candle power"), and appropriate carpeting and decor for color television. In short, the major networks and wireservices virtually moved to Miami Beach. Timothy Crouse (1972: 165) adequately described the scene.

> The conventions, however, were the greatest media events on earth. The convention hall was the world's biggest TV studio, lit for TV with 150 miles of electric cable, and with almost every public event staged expressly for TV. The networks dominated the conventions by sheer numbers. CBS had a staff of 500; NBC and ABC had 450 each . . . the conventions were really conventions of media people . . . the reporters spent a great deal of time interviewing each other about the coverage of the conventions.

Many newsmen, and probably most delegates, got the bulk of their knowledge about the conventions from the Associated Press, United Press International, newspapers, and televised network summaries.

I witnessed many examples of this media interplay. The most extensive use of other media involved relying on televised network summaries during the long hours of the Democratic Convention. Some newsmen refused to stay at the convention hall until 3:00 a.m. and chose to rely on network "wraps," while in the comfort of their hotel rooms, sipping drinks. A reporter could then write the story from his particular slant and meet a deadline at the home office via telephone. On several occasions I observed people reading newspaper articles which were originally based on either AP or network summaries of the days' events.

The interplay, if not circular exchange, between these media is most evident when it is inadequate. This occurred during the Miami mayor's address to the convention. A Miami reporter watched the network coverage from the AP photoroom, which was only feet away from the convention floor, because he did not have a floor pass. To his dismay, the networks did not present the speech, but instead switched back and forth across the floor to various reporters discussing assorted angles on the "big story." This newsman frantically cranked the channel selector and explained that he had to "top a story" in the morning paper and needed to know what was said before the competition told him the next day. This interdependency is one reason that the impressions of some media influence others.

NETWORK COVERAGE

The *most significant point* about network coverage of the conventions is that it was live. This was evident in the selection and coverage of events. Two of the three major networks provided "gavel-to-gavel" coverage, while ABC presented evening summaries. This extensive coverage created practical problems for the large number of reporters and support personnel who were oriented to covering newsworthy events susceptible toward the underlying angles of controversy, conflict, and drama.

Networks do not "turn the camera on the podium" for several reasons. Network producers believe that other important convention activities occur behind the scenes, on the floor, in caucuses, in hotel lobbies, and in the streets. While network officials have been criticized for covering such events—especially the street action of the 1968 Democratic Convention—most correspondents, I interviewed felt that omitting these scenes would mislead viewers since only part of the convention story would be presented. From this perspective, a more complete presentation consisted of switching from speeches in the hall to anchormen in the booths, to reporters on the floor, and to "remote" cameras stationed outside the hall.

Each camera "feeds" one of fourteen or more monitors in each network's control room. A producer coordinates the division of labor by scanning the monitors and selecting one to "go live," although others may be simultaneously taping. The effect is to transform the conventions into a series of discrete but related events, each becoming part of the producer's whole. An outcome of this organization, in part dictated by the reliance on network technology, is the definition of reality that suits broadcasting needs. Michael Shamberg, the head of a freelance effort to capture the conventions on small video tape machines, noted (Crouse, 1972: 182-183):

> The networks have never understood that the expensive equipment they have dictates a style, which is what's pissing people off. They have to force behavior. When they're on live, or even when they're filming, they have to have something happening when the camera's on. Everything they do costs so much that they can't afford to be patient. That's why they have correspondents who are always talking to give you the illusion that something's happening. They can't wait and really pick up on what's happening.

As noted above, the live coverage demands well-coordinated efforts and angles between the men in the booth and those in the field. Unlike the Channel B reporters, network correspondents were often directed by their booth superiors, who would select reports on the basis of how they fit into some ongoing story, or for a new emphasis that one of the directors had in mind. For example, a correspondent's suggestion that his network do a report on McGovern's inconsistency on certain rule interpretations was rejected by producers one day before another network "broke" the story. Perhaps the biggest disappointment was the decision not to interview Senator Eagleton the day before he was selected as McGovern's running mate. The correspondent's frustration was heightened when technical problems prevented live coverage at Eagleton's hotel when the decision was formally announced.

The extensive coverage, combined with the various camera locations, gives the booth coordinators the responsibility of deciding what is important enough to air. For these reasons, it is rare during convention coverage for a reporter to do a spontaneous report without time to get prepared. Two network reporters were instructed to prepare respective pieces on "substance" and "color." When one correspondent lapsed into "color," the booth producer screamed "he stole the story" from the other reporter, whose ad lib, would essentially repeat what had just been said, destroying the producer's plan for an organized report. A radio reporter's surprise about a quick decision to "go live" illustrates how common preparation time is.

> Is it going to be very long? Oh, two minutes, okay. I am going to do something live, good heavens. I don't know what the hell to talk about. Let's see, I haven't thought about anything about the convention but specific state issues . . . well, they want to do a live [transmission] on my observations of the convention at this hour, I actually have none . . . I think I can contrast it with what I saw last month at the Democratic Convention at this point.

Thus it can be seen that the reliance on advance warning is more apparent when it is not given.

The capacity to coordinate discrete events throughout the day transforms the convention activities into the world of news—each is likened to spontaneous occurrences which provide examples of controversy, conflict, drama, and a sense of importance.

But the conventions are different. Those who plan them know that conflict, etc., may make good news reports, but are not the sort of thing that serves the political party's interest; conflict is bad public relations and conventions are for exactly the opposite. As convention managers plan away controversy and disagreements, they are also wiping out potential news stories. The upshot is that a good convention from the standpoint of those who put it on is a bad convention for those who report it. The large number of news personnel will have less to do, or their assignments will not be as interesting and challenging, if the convention is staged and more controlled.

The consequences of not having enough newsworthy events to cover can be seen in the different assessments journalists made of the Democratic and Republican Conventions. Almost every news person I talked with felt the Democratic meeting was more interesting than the Republican. When the former opened, one writer called it "one of the most dramatic evenings in the colorful history of American politics" (Barrett, 1973: 120). The reason for this view is not hard to find. The Democrats' show was scripted and planned, but it did not go according to the prearranged directions. There were many "novice" delegates involved, and new platform planks were being considered, including abortion, a guaranteed income, and amnesty for draft resisters. This controversial material, and the publicized disagreements within the party over these programs, made the Democratic Convention good for news. This was not true of the Republican gathering.

Few journalists felt the Republican Convention had much that was newsworthy, with the exception of street demonstrations. Some even scolded me for suggesting that there was *anything* noteworthy about it! They were offended by the careful detailing away of any reasonable interpretations or conjectures not already implied by the official presentation. One writer's comment to a drinking buddy that he just had a feeling Agnew would not be Nixon's VP-designate, was answered with, "you're trying too hard; have another drink." In short, from a newsworker's perspective the Republicans had their act together in "the largest television studio in the world." The incorporation of Hollywood personalities, pomp and pageantry, and the split-second timing of important speeches to reach the prime-time television audience was viewed by most news personnel as a contrived event. This became more infuriating when the hall lights would be dimmed during film presentations, which discouraged network producers from switching to interviews with floor reporters. The Republicans' plan was to increase the likelihood that the cameras would carry the propaganda films to the viewing audience; thus, they were in control rather than the networks' booths. Halberstam (1976: 83) described the Republicans' strategy:

> They studied how the networks had covered previous national conventions, and they broke the code and wrote their own scenario. . . . All of it was perhaps boring, but better boredom than the chaos of earlier conventions. Control was of the essence.

As CBS correspondent Roger Mudd put it (Crouse, 1972: 176):

There really wasn't that much for a reporter to do down there if he was a television man and trapped on the floor. It was *arranged* so there wasn't much to do. You were a prisoner on that floor and everytime you got going on something they'd kill the house lights and roll the film so you couldn't broadcast anyhow.

The news situation was so grim that the lack of news became news when a misplaced Republican schedule found its way to ABC's newsroom. A reporter did a story emphasizing that "our suspicions" of planned "spontaneous events" were now confirmed. He went on to note the precise times that certain activities would occur, including the chairman's request to "clear the aisles."

In sum, the network coverage was informed by the amount of time to fill with newsworthy stories, and the presence or absence of events susceptible to news criteria. These considerations, along with the coordination and scheduling believed essential to complete convention coverage, discouraged investigative reporting and individual angles on various events. The capacity of the events to satisfy these prescriptions made them either good news or bad news.

LOCAL COVERAGE

Practical matters also informed how Channel B's news teams covered the conventions. However, their problems were different from those of the networks, and so was their coverage. Local news personnel shipped their film reports. This meant that "big stories" at the conventions would not be covered because the filmed reports would be dated by the time they arrived the next day; the networks' live broadcasts would date the local reports by at least hours. The local journalists' option was to concentrate on the local side of the conventions. This slant is illustrated by some of the stories at each convention.

Democratic:

  (1) a feature story on where the state delegation was staying (a very "out of the way place") and the high prices;

  (2) a story about a credential challenge that was written before the issue was resolved in order to meet a flight;

(3) an interview with two young delegates who had been featured in a brief promotional interview before leaving for the convention.

Republican:

(1) a filmed comment in front of the state delegation on the convention floor;

(2) eight potential gubernatorial candidates, filmed and talked about;

(3) a monologue about the party atmosphere and preparations for the Republican convention;

(4) an interview with the hometown chief of police who was visiting Miami Beach to observe how demonstrators and other convention incidents were handled.

Unlike their network colleagues who depended on the judgment and decisions of a booth coordinator for assignments, local reporters developed their own stories. This was done by developing an angle and then getting filmed evidence of it. For example, Channel B's reporter had thought, before his flight to Miami Beach, about how the conventions would be covered. Upon arrival at the hotel for the Republican Convention (which had already been defined as a non-news event) one of the reporters suggested that they do a story on the "party atmosphere," and the number of hospitality rooms set up to celebrate a "coronation." This story, like most of their projects, could have been done before or after the convention. However, Miami Beach did provide a scenic backdrop and the sense that "this is what conventions are all about." The use of the conventions as a context for news stories was most evident when the news team would rush onto the convention floor, collar a member of their state's delegation, and then get a few filmed comments, along with shots of balloons, network correspondents, and bright lights.

The use of angles to predefine a story helps resolve many practical problems, including getting enough stories done in time to air-freight film reports. However, it may also influence what a reporter sees. Upon his return from the convention, the Channel B reporter appeared on a news analysis show. He was asked to give the TV audience any firsthand impressions about demonstrations.

Well, it is hard to tell about the leadership situation; there were a number of Western City people that sort of played a key role, but a lot of different groups were doing a lot of different things; they have, you know, the hippies, and then they have the women's movement, and the Vietnam veterans against the war, and essentially *they all had their own leaders, and sometimes they seemed to have difficulty communicating with each other;* everyone had a different idea about what an action ought to be, and I think that may have had something to do with the way the demonstrations were conducted.

This reporter apparently saw this problem *eighth months earlier* and commented on it during a taped interview about the upcoming conventions.

They [demonstrators] don't have any guarantee that they will end up leading the convention demonstrations. . . . What happens when people do come in here and demonstrating and protesting . . . if there is a misunderstanding? *Who leads who and what kind of mechanism are they setting up within the ranks of the demonstrators for self-monitoring for communicating with authorities.*

These news reports were, for the most part, informed by practical constraints rather than firsthand involvement with events or careful analysis.

Local convention coverage, unlike the network national news, relied on filmed reports which were shipped to the home station. This discouraged local reporters from following the "big stories" that networks covered "live." But the requirement to ship one ot two stories about the convention each day promoted the use of predefined angles. This independence permitted reporters to do their jobs, but it also provided favorable evaluations of the conventions as news topics. Channel B's news teams agreed that the Republican Convention was not as interesting as the Democratic, but they nevertheless saw both as good assignments, especially when their stories took them to the convention floor, the "thick of news . . . right beside the network 'heavies.' "

Summary

The news coverage of the 1972 National Political Conventions accentuates the problems and procedures of all newswork. Events were approached with practical understandings about the available means to transform them into news. The different constraints on network and local TV news prompted distinctive reports. Despite these differences, one essential similarity remained. All news personnel I encountered explicitly or implicitly understood that news practices promote—and often depend on—wrenching an event from its context in order to tell a story about it. But other people, like convention managers, have caught on to this tendency. Political organizers have believed for years that the mass media are the key to political success or failure, and this belief has led them to stage the conventions as a kind of advertising show in which candidates and party aims are reunited with the founding fathers of the country. The organizers' inability to control all facets of of the widely publicized convention events permits outsiders to define the situation. This loss of control, and its effects, were most clearly seen during the coverage of the street fighting at the 1968 Democratic Convention in Chicago, as well as of parts of the Democratic meeting in 1972. In each case, spontaneity was evident, authority was defied, arguments were brought out into the open, and the media did their work. But, as noted above, what is good work for them is often disaster for those whose stories are being worked on. The election results in both 1968 and 1972 would seem not to contradict this interpretation. It is difficult for both media agents to do "good" work at the same time. This is why the conflict between public actors and journalists is likely to increase.

Chapter 6

THE EAGLETON AND

WATERGATE STORIES

The political conventions were not the only major news stories in 1972. The Eagleton story, and the first reports about the now infamous Watergate break-in, dominated the news. Both stories had tremendous social and political consequences. In the Eagleton case, a man selected to be the Democratic vice presidential nominee was forced to resign following extensive press—and editorial— coverage of his revelation that he had been treated for mental illness. The Watergate story, in the early stages, involved burglars and buggers with White House connections. More than two years of news reports, and subsequent uncovering of other White House irregularities, led to the indictment and jailing of a number of White House aides, and the resignation of President Nixon. The impact of these stories on the fate of the people involved invites analysis, but there is a more important reason for assessing what role, if any, the news perspective played in these news reports.

One issue is bias. A popular view among journalists and others is that ideological commitment, or political persuasion, is the most significant source of bias. According to this view, one side finds its way into news reports and tends to color the facts that are *presented,* but more often, influences the way facts are *interpreted.*

For example, Frank Mankiewicz, McGovern's campaign manager during the 1972 campaign, was quite distraught with the coverage given the Eagleton story. Mankiewicz was very critical of the news process during a televised discussion on NBC on September 26, 1972:

> NBC has apparently decided that a fit subject for another panel to discuss is the media treatment of what you call the Eagleton affair. That seems to me an example of at best subconscious bias at work. I never heard any discussion of the media treatment of that as particularly good or bad. It seems to me it will work unfairly to the Democratic campaign. There are events, for example, the Watergate affair, there is the whole question of about how the media has handled charges of corruption in the Nixon administration that never get discussed that would be equally unfair.

Advocates of this approach to media bias see the solution in balanced reporting, that is, giving both sides of an issue, or in the long run permitting all sides (usually two) to have an equal amount of newspaper space, or in the case of TV news, equivalent air time.

Since this kind of bias is the most well known, it is the one people look for the most, not realizing that other forms of bias may be operating. I refer to the bias of the news perspective which selects and examines events in accordance with scheduling, presentational, and other practical demands, including the necessity to tell a story within a very short time. Part of this perspective is the routine use of themes, or general characterizations of events over a period of time. These general definitions may, in some news reports, be updated or reinforced with angles or more specific encapsulating ideas. Despite their usefulness to those reporting the news, such recipes often prevent a fuller understanding of the events that are being reported. And this bias can operate independently of ideological and/or political leanings. Thus, the Democrats and Republicans both suffered at the hands of newsworkers, and this *may* indicate that news agents were not letting their political inclinations influence what they reported. But that does not mean there were not other systematic biases at work, which may have distorted events in a nonpartisan way. In a sense, then, I am seeking to control for political influence in the news process by including a Democratic and Republican defeat by the press. The intent is to further establish the workings of the news perspective and its impact. Also, the coverage of each of these stories drew praise from the journalism fraternity. Examining what the news contributed to these stories affords a glance at the criteria newsworkers invoke in sanctioning the quality of collegial performance.

The Eagleton Case

When Senator Thomas Eagleton was selected as the Democratic vice presidential nominee on July 13, 1972, a network field producer said, "We'll give him good exposure on TV. . . . Agnew has had it." The exposure began on July 25, when Eagleton announced that he had "checked myself into hospitals three times in the 1960s for nervous exhaustion and fatigue and twice underwent electric-shock treatments." A great deal of media attention was focused on this disclosure, amounting to thousands of column inches in newspapers and several hours on both network and local television newscasts. Such coverage played an important part in McGovern's revocation of his "irrevocable 1000 percent" backing of his vice presidential nominee. By July 31, Eagleton had been unceremoniously dropped as the number two Democratic standard-bearer. Following this announcement, Senator McGovern said,

> We didn't know the impact on the country . . . as the days went on, it became clear to me that Senator Eagleton's past medical history, not the state of his health today, which I think is excellent, which his doctors say is excellent, but *his past medical history has literally dominated the news*. . . . I was of the opinion that this issue would continue to plague the campaign.

McGovern's dismay was matched by Eagleton's surprise at the amount of news coverage his history received.

Quite frankly, I did not think the experience I had in these instances
[of depression] was of that great moment. *I now realize it is. I've read
the headlines in the morning papers.*

How such disclosure had the impact of "that great moment"
invites scrutiny of the process which made Eagleton's story.

THE EAGLETON STORY

The Eagleton case received extensive news coverage for several
reasons. First, the period between the Democratic and Republican
Conventions is famous for being "slow for news." This is because
the conventions are considered the top news stories, and the
important political figures are generally so enmeshed in organizing
and cleaning up last-minute details that they are making relatively
few public appearances or statements. In short, newsworkers are
not likely to look elsewhere for news, and they find little when
they do search (White, 1973: 275). After the story broke, and
Eagleton returned to being a senator instead of a vice presidential
hopeful, a network anchorman commented in a personal interview
about the relevance of "slow news" to this story.

Anchorman: It was objective. There is a problem in journalism which is that
    journalism is keyed, it's built up to cover the crises, to cover the war,
    to cover the disasters. Therefore when you get a relatively placid
    period, when you get a dramatic development, I think we probably
    overreact, we overreact objectively, it's just a matter of a bunch of
    people trying to get a story.

D.A.: Oh excuse me, by placid period, what . . . ?

Anchorman: Well, McGovern is nominated, it's the interlude between the
    conventions, there's not great news going on. We would normally
    be covering the campaign, so I think there is some overreaction.
    But I think the overreaction is better than any kind of controlled
    reaction.

After it was all over, Senator Eagleton conceded that the amount
of coverage was probably influenced by "a slow news week."

I'm certainly no longer Tom Who. I guess I'm for the moment in the top
twenty in the country in terms of name identification as a practicing

office holder. Some of my notoriety, I think will fade. I won't be a
very hot news item, maybe a week from now unless I give them a good
speech on the floor of the Senate [CBS, August 1, 1972].

One month after Eagleton's dismissal, and two months before the
election, a writer for the *New Republic* observed,

Although I think individual reporters played it very straight, the total
thing was a kind of circus, and I don't know how to explain it. I think
it has something to do with there not being any other news that week,
or something like that. But the total thing was very bad [NBC, September 26, 1972].

Eagleton was the *best* story around partly because he was the *only*
story. It was also important that very little was known about him.
Unlike other politicians of whom a great deal is known, but little
reported, Eagleton was unknown to most reporters who covered
him. This meant that their task was to find something interesting
about Eagleton. An interview with one reporter who was involved
in breaking the story illustrates the preoccupation with finding
something newsworthy—that is, something previously unknown
or spectacular. A reporter assigned to do a profile on Eagleton
was told about a telephone call from a McGovern supporter
who wanted to protect McGovern from a less than candid running mate. This informant was concerned that Eagleton's history
of mental illness and shock therapy may be used against the
Democrats by the Republicans. In a subsequent call, the informer
offered the name of a hospital where Eagleton had received
psychiatric treatment and also provided the name of the super-
vising physician. When questioned by the reporter, however, the
physician refused to provide much information, although his "no
comment" response had specific meanings for the experienced
journalist.

Reporter: I drove out there and talked to the doctor who wouldn't talk
to me, but in not talking to me it was pretty strong confirmation
that it was so because, you know, if you come up to somebody's
door and knock on it and say, gee, I hear you were present when
Senator Eagleton had shock therapy in 1960 at Renard Hospital,

you know, if it's not the truth you say it's not true, you're crazy
[laughs]. Instead the response was I won't talk to you about that
[personal field notes].

Discovering a background of hospitalization and treatment is
one thing, but it is another to sense that the history is being
hidden. Denials of this past may suggest that the candidate has
a "credibility problem," a big story for any reporter. The credibility angle was the foundation for Jack Anderson's charges that
Eagleton had "been arrested for drunken and reckless driving."
Anderson's (1974: 185) pursuit of the story began with the belief
that the drunk driving charge "was a simple test of Eagleton's
credibility that could be resolved, clearly and in time to be serv-
iceable"—that is, get him off the ticket. He felt that photostats of
drunken driving arrests would be enough evidence to raise questions about Eagleton's credibility since Anderson was convinced
the Missouri Senator had lied to McGovern and had conspired to
make his psychiatric records inaccessible. Another reporter explained how he obtained subsequent information about the Eagleton case:

> We touched other sources, you know, this is a kind of delicate area.
> We talked to some psychiatric sources, who also would not say any-
> thing specific but also, like the first physician tended to deal in terms
> that were couched so that it was a tacit confirmation. . . . In some
> cases we would be very generally asking questions about how one
> would go about getting information in very broad general terms trying
> to pinpoint a name, and after a few questions, in one case the guy said,
> are you talking about a vice presidential candidate? In another case
> somebody said, are you talking about the man from Missouri [personal
> field notes] ?

The final reason for the Eagleton story—regarded by some journalists as the "most spectacular of the year"—was that mental
illness was relatively unique as a news topic. This warrants emphasis. Mental illness had been long familiar to broadcasters as entertainment and to others as scientific information (Nunnally, 1961;
Tannenbaum, 1963), but it had never before been treated as a
major news story. What made it newsworthy was that a vice presidential nominee "had it," one who, according to one detractor,

could "have his finger on the [nuclear] button." The larger issue for those who broke the story, and subsequently forced Eagleton's public disclosure (White, 1973: 268), was the lack of any precedent in handling this type of unfavorable background information. For example, untoward behavior such as excessive drinking and aberrant sexual practices by men in public office is known about, but seldom reported unless the police blotter is splotched—as in the case of Edward Kennedy on Chappaquiddick. Mental illness was viewed differently. The ensuing problem for journalists was suggested by one newspaperman's comment:

> What about the violation of privacy? . . . There is a gentlemen's agreement in the press that a man's sex life and his drinking . . . is [sic] not mentioned by the press until it hits the police blotter. . . . It does not become a major factor reported by newsmen though newsmen know everything about the sex lives of men in high office and the drinking habits. Where do we draw the line on . . . psychotherapy [NBC, September 26, 1972]?

The Eagleton case became a news story and received the kind of coverage it did, for various reasons. The slow news period encouraged journalists to search for news. Eagleton's newly won national attention, the discovery of his history of mental illness, and questions about his credibility provided the specific angles for news coverage, but one theme tied them together: Eagleton had to be dropped as the Democratic vice presidential nominee. While this dominant theme provided continuity for most day-to-day news reports, it was especially true of television coverage. Excerpts and summaries from the CBS newscasts for the week of July 26 to August 1, 1972, illustrate the theme of dumping Eagleton.

> *July 26:* Reporters emphasize that many party workers are concerned that Eagleton's disclosures may hurt the campaign—e.g., "There is now the unknown ingredient; to what degree will the Senator's past affect his future." Major party leaders—e.g., Kennedy—are supportive of Eagleton, but the reporter asks about procedures for selecting a replacement.
>
> *July 27:* Newspaper editorials calling for Eagleton's resignation are cited. It is reported that McGovern is cautious: "But despite all the denials,

it is clear that . . . dropping Eagleton from the ticket is still very much alive." Jack Anderson charges that Eagleton had been cited for drunken driving.

July 28: Viewers are told that the New York *Times* is the last major newspaper to call for Eagleton's resignation. Eagleton's adamant denial of Anderson's charges is reported to show that "the controversy surrounding him is growing [but] Senator Eagleton himself is showing fewer signs of strain than when it began. Before it is over he will have demonstrated to what degree he has learned to handle stress." The chief counsel for the Democratic National Committee is asked about the procedure for picking another candidate.

July 29: McGovern is reported to be under intense pressure to dump Eagleton, despite McGovern's insistence to the contrary. Eagleton claims the public "is with me." The reporter concludes with "Senator Eagleton is still signing autographs and shaking hands like a candidate, but doubts remain as to whether he will be doing so by this time next week."

July 30: The news opens with, "Indications are growing tonight that Democratic presidential candidate Senator George McGovern is trying to get Senator Thomas Eagleton to quit as his running mate." Eagleton is asked in an interview if he can assure the people that he can withstand the pressures of office. His answer that he can give the same assurance as the Republican candidates is met with, "But they don't have your past record, do they?" Party Chairwoman Jean Westwood reverses her earlier support of Eagleton on a network talk show with, "It would be the noble thing for Tom Eagleton to step down." A CBS special report on the Eagleton case reviews the week's news and notes how much publicity his disclosure has attracted.

July 31: A sense of conflict is reported between the McGovern and Eagleton "camps." Replacements for Eagleton are discussed after reporting that "the McGovern-Eagleton ticket is still intact this morning with a lot of guessing that it won't stay that way very long." Eric Sevareid comments, "The two men [McGovern and Eagleton] have trapped themselves [and] political blood will flow."

August 1: It is reported that "the bottom dropped out for Senator Thomas Eagleton." During a thirty-minute interview Eagleton denies that he was "forced off the ticket." A reporter tells Eagleton, "I know you saw this past week as a test, as a way to answer all those questions about your health." Jack Anderson retracts his charges about Eagleton's citations for drunken driving. Reporters agree that never has there been a "vice presidential affair as exciting, as unusual, as headline-making as this one." The process for selecting a replacement is discussed. Eric Sevareid comments that "fire started by the press is very hot fire, but in the long run it is cleansing."

Newsworkers were preoccupied with presenting the Eagleton story. The total picture became more important than the specifics, which were interpreted within the broader theme. One of the first reporters to become aware of the Eagleton case explained how he did some of the initial groundwork.

> You get a little tiny piece here and a little tiny piece there . . . no huge dramatic moment when a light-bulb went on . . . just little pieces keep coming and then finally I sat down at a typewriter and wrote about a seven-page memo . . . looking at it and seeing where these things fit [personal field notes].

However, as the story developed, the procedures for putting it all together were forgotten; it took on an objective aura. This was expressed in a CBS report, "The Eagleton Case" (July 30, 1972).

> Already the issues have gone from shock treatment, to Eagleton's candor, to McGovern's judgment, to the meeting tomorrow [between Eagleton and McGovern].... How they deal with each other from now on will shape the campaign and influence the election; it will tell us a good deal more about them than we know—perhaps even more than they know themselves.

These reporters could have added that it will also tell us a good deal about the news process.

Reporters were not interested in clarifying the nature of mental illness, although they did consult "experts" who emphasized how difficult it was to be certain whether complete recovery had occurred. One reporter who broke the story expected Eagleton to have his physicians testify to his recovery, especially since "he was fighting with everything he had." The lack of sworn testimony suggested to this journalist, and to Jack Anderson, that maybe the attending medical people were not really certain how capable Eagleton was. When asked whether Eagleton's performance during the strenuous "week that was" attested to his stability, the reporter said no. He willingly admitted that Eagleton had come through some very difficult periods, but that didn't really raise any serious questions because we could not be sure how Eagleton would handle a prolonged crisis like the Cuban missile situation, especially when he had access to nuclear buttons. Moreover, he felt that the depression and nervous exhaustion for which Eagleton had just been treated were "symptoms and not the problem itself." A network reporter raised the same issue in an interview (CBS, July 30, 1972; see the chronology given above). This reporter's understanding of mental illness was far removed from medical (cf. Chase, 1973: 8-11) and current social-psychological perspectives which emphasize that symptoms are defined—and treated—by others as illness, and that one is indistinguishable without the other (cf. Szasz, 1961, 1970; Scheff, 1966, 1967, 1974: 444-452).

Mental illness, shock therapy, and "credibility problems" offered different ways of presenting the dominant theme that Eagleton was a political liability and that the story was still unfolding. Pursuing these angles in order to obtain more evidence discouraged journalists from finding out how well Eagleton could handle questions about issues such as the Vietnam war, civil rights, tax reform, and the like. These avenues would seem to be more plausible routes to a candidate's capacity to meet the challenges of his office, but they were hardly considered in the face of the dominant theme. Virtually every question Eagleton was asked pertained to his shaky tenure as a candidate. After he announced his medical past, a writer for the New York *Times* wrote, "Mr. Eagleton himself was manifestly nervous—his hands and his face seeming to quiver slightly." A similar fate awaited Eagleton's appearance on a network talk show when a correspondent suggested that he seemed nervous.

While reporters were finding his case to be the most interesting vice presidential affair in history, Eagleton was befuddled at all the coverage.

It was sort of my personal belief that the Eagleton issue would fade away through this month of August. . . . I thought that [CBS reporter] would get tired of asking me in every city of the country about my health, and that it would run its course [CBS, August 1, 1972].

He was also puzzled at the kind of coverage he was getting.

> Those who had a negative side are some who we think of as being more
> sophisticated, by that I mean the editorial pages of some of the more
> sophisticated newspapers. They take the position that the previous ill-
> ness would disbar me from seeking higher office. . . . I would have felt
> that the public on the whole would be rather suspicious or negative,
> but I would have thought that the editorial page of, say, the New York
> *Times* or the Washington *Post* would have been much more understand-
> ing, so in my judgment I was 180 degrees wrong on what the reaction
> would be [NBC, September 26, 1972].

The apparent lack of sophistication can be traced to the news
perspective rather than to a lack of understanding. Even though
news agents rate high on Nunnally's (1961: 215) predictor of
sophistication and toleration of mental health (i.e., formal education), they produced unsophisticated coverage because they
were guided by their working perspective, and they were not the
only ones.

THE BELIEF IN NEWS

Senator Eagleton offered to quit the ticket on the same day he
publicized his bout with depression, his exhaustion, and his subsequent hospitalization. When McGovern refused this offer, Eagleton
insisted he would resign if he sensed that the public was against
his candidacy on the Democratuc ticket. He also stated that he
would look to the public opinion polls before making his final
decision. We shall see that the Democratic leadership placed a
great deal of confidence in the news agencies' ability to read—and
possibly direct—public opinion.

Eagleton's registers of public opinion were basically encouraging. He told one reporter,

> I'm not kidding about this. The people are with me on this . . . they
> were hugging me. Kissing me. Grabbing my hand. While I was trying
> to swim in the lake, one elderly woman came up to me, gave me a big
> bear hug and said, 'Hang in there, kid! [Newsweek, August 7, 1972].

The opinion polls also failed to show overwhelming public dissatisfaction with Eagleton. The Gallup poll recorded majorities of roughly two to one in favor of Eagleton remaining on the ticket, although nearly one third of the independent voters felt this might influence their decision to vote against Democrats. *Time*'s (August 7, 1972) survey of 1,105 eligible voters found that McGovern had not lost more than one and one-half percent of the vote due to Eagleton. The news coverage was not as equivocal as the polls.

We have already seen that the television coverage emphasized the theme that Eagleton would be dropped. Newspapers went beyond merely publicizing the Eagleton story; they advocated that Eagleton leave the ticket, and they forecast doom if he remained. A writer for the New York *Times* felt the public pulse and told about in on July 27:

> It is also doubtful whether new attitudes have taken sufficient hold that the public would be willing to accept the idea that a man cured of mental illness would be capable of withstanding the strains of the White House—whether he would be stable enough, to use the phrase often heard from voters, 'to have his finger on the button.'

The *Times* printed the New York City Democratic Chairman's statement urging Eagleton to withdraw "in order to maintain confidence in our governmental and political structure."

The Eagleton issue overshadowed any other aspect of the campaign coverage, but the "public interest" was most directly presented in the editorial pages. McGovern is reported to have told Eagleton that he had "thirty editorials here in my hand which are against you" (White, 1973: 271). These views were also couched in the public interest. The liberal New York *Post* was among the first (July 26) calling for Eagleton's resignation.

> His continued presence on the ticket can only produce cruel diversionary conflict in a year when real issues should sharply be defined and debated. . . . We believe that Eagleton should withdraw.

The Washington *Post* concurred the next day.

It is our judgment that the burden imposed by the presence of Senator Eagleton on the ticket can only be removed by his withdrawal as a candidate.

The Baltimore *Evening Sun*'s point that Eagleton "has been refreshingly candid, courageous and convincing," was offset by the *Morning Sun*'s editorial:

Eagleton should promptly resign the nomination out of a sense of proper respect toward Senator George McGovern, the Democratic Party, and most important, the American people.

The Los Angeles *Times* was another major newspaper pursuing the public interest.

Eagleton looks like a serious political liability for McGovern. It is hard to see how McGovern and Eagleton can avoid the conclusion that it would be best for Eagleton to withdraw.

Finally, after taking several days to assess the situation, on July 28 the New York *Times* made it unanimous among the large-circulation papers. After noting that the real issues had been clouded by the Eagleton case, and that the pressures he experienced as senator were miniscule compared to those of the presidency, the conclusion was:

It would be a helpful contribution not only to the McGovern candidacy but to the health of the American political process for Senator Eagleton to retire from the field and permit the Presidential contest to be decided only on the issues.

If that was not enough, another scribe wrote in the *Times* on the same day:

There was never any chance that a question of mental depression treated by electric shock would be dropped, even on the recommendation of doctors, who differ with other doctors, on the problem. . . . The resignation of Mr. Eagleton is probably the least damaging way out of the mess.

These were the editorial directions, but how were they regarded by the McGovern staff? I do not claim to provide a definitive answer to this question, but it is not too difficult to show that these powerful messages had some impact.

McGovern, his staff, and many reporters felt that the Eagleton story would influence the campaign. There were two reasons for this: First, they believed there was no way to avoid the story as long as Eagleton remained a candidate; and second, they felt resulting news coverage would sway voters. Following Eagleton's departure from the ticket, McGovern commented on the news coverage.

[I] was of the opinion that this issue would continue to plague the campaign. Ladies and gentlemen, look at the press, at the news, at the magazines. This has been the issue that has blotted out the war, blotted out the economy, blotted out all the central questions before the nation [CBS, August 1, 1972].

Eagleton concurred that the reports about his health had not subsided in the way he hoped, and he discussed this when questioned about the decisive meeting he had with McGovern.

He expressed his confidence in me. He expressed satisfaction that my health was adequate, but he pointed out—and an argument can be made on this side—that if I remained on the ticket all the tension and all the debate would be about Eagleton ... 'his past medical history,' and it would take away from focusing on some problems that have to be attended to: the Vietnam war, the economy, the credibility gap, etc., the important issues that he must debate and should debate [CBS, August 1, 1972].

Why the issue would linger on was a question many people knew the answer to, but dared not to say. The news media were responsible for the Eagleton story, but party officials knew the press could not be criticized for it; to do so could produce a story about censorship. Indeed, the press's treatment of the Eagleton case was cited by Eric Sevareid as evidence that the journalism profession was not one-sided.

And there's an ancillary lesson in the events of the past week. They cast doubt on the Nixon-Agnew conviction that the so-called liberal press will always give the Democrats, and McGovern in particular, the benefit of the doubt. It was the big liberal organs of the press that held McGovern's feet to the fire, that scrutinized his conduct the most severely [CBS, August 1, 1972].

When Eagleton was asked if he thought "the people of the United States are actually not that concerned, but that the press seems to be going crazy over it?," he replied, "Hey, that's pretty good! No. No, I think the press is very well mentally balanced." Several days after this television interview, and one day prior to Eagleton's resignation, another reporter raised the publicity issue in a filmed interview (CBS, July 30, 1972).

Eagleton: I think that I was known as "Tom Who?" up until a week ago and perhaps my contribution to the ticket might be plus one or plus one-and-a-half. I think with this publicity [I] am a plus rather than the minus . . . earlier in the week.

Reporter: But that's not the kind of publicity you really want, is it? The jokes that follow you about, a 'shocking' good time and a 'brilliant' this, and having to explain on national television about your drinking.

Eagleton: I had no drinking problem.

Reporter: No, but they keep coming up. Always on the defensive; that is not the way to run for Vice President.

Eagleton: No. I think in due course, meaning in a reasonably foreseeable period of time, that the Eagleton issue will fade away after I've answered the questions time, and time, and time again so that they become boresomely repetitious, the news value will have been gone and we'll get about the discussion of the real issues, and I don't think this will take as long as some people think. I think it can be done in a period of a week or ten days.

It comes as no surprise that the candidates felt somewhat helpless about their inability to control the issues and what was defined as news, but it is interesting that the newsworkers also felt they had little choice. This determined view of news was expressed by a newspaper editor several months after the Eagleton story lost its news value.

I don't know what your definition of news is. If the candidate for vice president finds himself in the situation that McGovern and Eagleton found themselves, my God, where do you want us to play it, with ads? It is a news event of importance [NBC, September 26, 1972].

From this perspective, the news coverage would have to treat Eagleton's mental illness and credibility as a liability as long as he remained in the national political spotlight. When Eagleton finally quit, several news organs agreed that the wise decision would let the "focus . . . shift back to a clarification by both presidential candidates of their approach to these issues."

The apparent irony of the news media's failure to perceive how they reacted to their previous definitions of Eagleton, mental illness, and the public interest, is dispelled when viewed from the news perspective. Newsworkers, and especially network and national reporters, are not unsophisticated regarding issues like mental illness and are generally liberal in their views toward more toleration, therapy, and understanding. Nevertheless, the search for an interesting thematic line on which to hang specific angles during a slow news period was enough to transform Eagleton's reluctant disclosure into "media overkill." Thus, pursuing the story was far more important than understanding what the events were about. According to one writer.

A great opportunity [was lost] to listen, and test the maturity of the American public on an issue ·that we never tried to sort of toss out to them. . . . We had a chance to test their sophistication and to wait for maybe two weeks to see how far we've come on this issue and . . . do some very, very good reporting on the realities of mental health, mental illness, and hospitalization [but] all that was lost in the tumult [NBC, September 26, 1972].

In brief, the Eagleton case was reconstructed as a news story. The news media not only publicized aspects of the Eagleton case, but the meaning of certain events was fundamentally altered in order to tell a story. The Eagleton case involved innumerable features of one man's biography, including: a father and husband, a Missouri politician, a U.S. senator, a vice presidential nominee, a series of hospitalizations for mental depression and exhaustion, the failure to tell McGovern about the latter, and so forth. Each of these experiences was more or less independent of the others and could affect his future in innumerable ways. However, it is the newsworker's task to tell a story about such discrete events by treating facts as evidence of a theme which provides continuity and gives a clear meaning. The resulting story was about Eagleton's impending resignation, a theme amplified by the angles of credibility, shock therapy, and mental illness. The incongruity between the meanings of Eagleton's experiences and the putative meanings of the story suggests that the news process in general, and especially television news practices, are media in their own right and are not merely messages transmitted over "hot" and "cool" channels, as McLuhan (1964) and others have claimed. While the form of communication may influence the message, the Eagleton story was constructed through emphasis, ommission, interpretation, and presentation—a filtering process which changed the meaning of the candidate's past and made certain events more newsworthy, and therefore more likely to be publicized. But this was not the only consequence of the news perspective.

The leaders of the Democratic Party were convinced that voters would be negatively influenced by the stories about Eagleton's mental health history and his lack of candor. This kind of publicity became a key aspect of Eagleton's political fate because the party bosses could not afford to campaign defensively by justifying why Eagleton should remain on the ticket. The only way to stop the "bad press" was to remove the target—Eagleton. This is how news practices contributed to the Democrats' problems.

Watergate

Without doubt the major news story of this decade is the constellation of events which has come to be known as Watergate. It is similar in several ways to the Eagleton reports. Both stories deal with events that occurred in 1972. One reason the major thrust of the Watergate developments did not break until the final months of 1972 is that the Eagleton story dominated the news for several weeks. A second, and even more important similarity between these stories, is the way they were shaped by the news perspective.

On June 17, 1972, five men associated with the Committee to Re-Elect the President (CREEP) were caught attempting to burglarize and bug the headquarters of the Democratic National Committee in the Watergate office-apartment-hotel complex. Subsequent investigation revealed that the funding and authorization for this act came from White House aides. While awaiting the trial of the "plumbers" (so-called because they were originally assembled to stop news "leaks") several aides to President Nixon planned a strategy to avoid major difficulties. From their perspective, the problem would gradually disappear. In a telephone conversation with John Mitchell on September 15, 1972, Nixon said (New York *Times,* 1973: 61):

> I was just sitting here with John Dean and he tells me you were going to be sued or something. Good, good, yeah, good, sure. Well. I tell you just don't let this keep you or your colleagues from concentrating on the big game. This thing is just one of those issues and a month later everybody looks back and wonders what all the shooting was about.

White House Counsel John Dean added:

> Three months ago I would have had trouble predicting there would be a day when this would be forgotten, but I think I can say that 54 days from now nothing is going to come crashing down to our surprise.

On February 28, 1972, Dean added:

> We have come a long road on this thing now, I had thought it was an impossible task to hold together until after the election until things started falling out, but we have made it this far and I am convinced we are going to make it the whole road and put this thing in the funny pages of the history books rather than anything serious.

They were wrong. Less than two years later, almost the entire White House staff was in jail or under indictment, and President Nixon resigned the position he won with the largest landslide in American history in order to avoid being impeached for obstruction of justice, misusing the FBI, CIA, and IRS, and non-compliance with Judiciary Committee requests for subpoenaed tapes and other documents. His public support, as indicated by Gallup polls, fell from sixty-eight percent in January 1973 to thirty-one percent in August, a new low for recent presidents.

That this should occur to an administration headed by a man acclaimed to be one of the country's shrewdest politicians seems strange. Especially since this holocaust began with what Nixon's own press secretary described as a "third-rate burglary attempt." To a man who had survived extreme political setbacks and opposition, and who had fought an uphill battle all the way to the White House, resolving a problem with intelligence procedures seemed minor indeed (cf. Vidich, 1975). And it would have been only an inconvenience if the news had not publicized other particulars, and most importantly, presented them as a unity.

The power of the press in the Watergate story has already been acknowledged, but the emphasis has been on the widespread publicity of the break-in, which in turn spurred other journalists to get in on the action, and finally, a congressional investigation got under way. Theodore H. White (1973: 327) has correctly noted the contribution of the news media to this and other issues.

> The power of the press in America is a primordial one. It sets the agenda of public discussion; and this sweeping political power is unrestrained by any law. It determines what people will talk and think about—an authority that in other nations is reserved for tyrants, priests, parties and mandarins.

> No major Act of the American Congress, no foreign adventure, no act of diplomacy, no great social reform can succeed in the United States unless the press prepares the public mind. And when the press seizes a great issue to thrust onto the agenda of talk, it moves action on its own—the cause of the environment, the cause of civil rights, the liquidation of the war in Vietnam, and, as climax, the Watergate affair were all set on the agenda, in the first instance, by the press.

White (1973: 398) has also accurately described what occurred following the early investigations by reporters from the Washington *Post,* CBS, and the New York *Times.*

> By the spring of 1973, long after the campaign was over, the press was swooping and wheeling over the bodies of the Nixon administration, without mercy or compassion, in full-pack cry; and as the administration seemed to be coming apart, every man who had a part in it was

made a target for whatever charge, whatever allegation, could be milked from whatever source. The outcry, the tumult, the juiciness of personalities and details was to make of Watergate a story outrunning in its continuous headlines and excitement even the outbreak of World War II.

This media overkill topicalized wrongdoing in the White House as a major issue. It was this exposure, White (1975: 224) suggests, plus the judicial system, and congressional leadership which led to the decline and fall of the Nixon administration. Frank Mankiewicz (1975: 83) agrees with this interpretation.

The press played a major role in the downfall of Nixon, but only because the news *happened* day after day and the papers and television reported it. . . . Once the official institutions began doing their job in the spring of 1973, it was a downhill race for the press and, to be sure, the 'media' [italics in original].

The implication of this view is that the presidential deeds were troublesome in some objective sense, and the facts spoke for themselves. The function of the press, according to this interpretation, was to serve as a channel in broadcasting the news, and *not* influence the reports. In the words of Frank Mankiewicz (1975: 88):

It was events which made the news, and not—as Nixon would like to remember it—the other way 'round. In Emerson's phrase, 'things are in the saddle, and ride mankind.'

So objectively wrong were Nixon's deeds that Mankiewicz sees Watergate as less a "political event" or "crisis" than a "legal proceeding," brought about by hard evidence. If this were true, then the illegal deeds of past presidents, including those who gave us the Vietnam war, would have made news, and their political life would have been cut short. The now public and sordid use of the FBI, IRS, and other government agencies by Presidents Johnson and Kennedy to bug and harrass members of "suspicious" groups was known by legislators and journalists alike, but no indictments were brought, no articles of impeachment written, and no administration destroyed.

The same can be said of the fears, moral crusades, and countless problems which confront us all. If the things people worry about were objectively obvious, then people would worry far more about being killed in an auto accident than about being mugged—but they do not; citizens and legislators would be more concerned with consumer fraud and massive corporate irregularities than with "crime in the streets"—but they are not; and fewer people would be concerned about children battered by parents than the thousands who are killed and maimed each year because car manufacturers and parents have not provided adequate safety systems. The disproportionate concern with one issue rather than another is more a feature of the publicity and news coverage each receives, and the way such stories are told than of their objective character.

The occurrence of certain events is one thing, but our knowledge and definitions of them is something else. This is true in our everyday affairs, and it is true with the public perception of the presidency. White (1975: 322-324) is correct in his assessment of the impact the Watergate revelations had on the presidency.

> All civilizations rest on myths, but in America myths have exceptional leaning. . . . Of all the political myths out of which the Republic was born, however, none was more hopeful than the crowning myth of the Presidency—that the people, in their shared wisdom, would be able to choose the best man to lead them. From this came a derivative myth— that the Presidency, the supreme office, would make noble any man who held its responsibility. . . . That myth held for almost two centuries. . . . Within all the myths, thus, the myth of the Presidency was crucial to the action against Richard Nixon. Many stupid, hypocritical and limited men had reached that office. But all, when publicly summoned to give witness, chose to honor the legends—or, if they had to break with them, broke only to meet a national emergency. Richard Nixon behaved otherwise. His lawlessness exploded the legends. He left a nation, approaching the 200th anniversary of its glorious independence, with a President and a Vice-President neither of whom had been chosen by the people. The faith was shattered.

But he is wrong in suggesting that Nixon was punished because he overstepped his bounds farther than any other president. *I suggest that Nixon fell from power because the news perspective transformed the series of events known as Watergate into a whole, which was then used as evidence of corruption and immorality.* Examining the context of the Watergate break-in, and the thrust of new reports, clarifies this view.

WATERGATE IN CONTEXT

Views of reality are taken for granted by the public and must be considered as an important context to consider in proposing solutions to fight crime, solve the drug problem, and the like. By the same token, President Nixon was operating in the historical context of increasing presidential power and related taken for granted prerogatives. In the words of historian Arthur M. Schlesinger, Jr. (1973: ix):

> By the early 1970's the American President had become on issues of war and peace the most absolute monarch (with the possible exception of Mao Tse-tung of China) among the great powers of the world. . . . And if the President were conceded these life-and-death decisions abroad, how could he be restrained from gathering unto himself the less fateful powers of the national polity.

This was the period after Lyndon Johnson pursued an illegal and undeclared war in Vietnam which cost several billions of dollars and hundreds of thousands of lives. No legal action was taken against him. And nothing was done to Richard Nixon when he continued to escalate this war and ordered massive bombing raids over Cambodia—an illegal act which also cost millions of dollars and took thousands of lives. It should be noted that the Committee on the Judiciary of the House of Representatives did not include this act as one of the articles of impeachment because they feared it would not pass! In short, they would impeach a president for the "obstruction of justice" on an intelligence-gathering operation, but not for making war without congressional approval! In this context, it is no wonder that Nixon saw only minor—if any—consequences from his role in the Watergate bungling. Professor Schlesinger (1973: ix-x) suggests that this was but an extension of a policy already set in motion.

> The all-purpose invocation of 'national security,' the insistence on executive secrecy, the withholding of information from Congress, the refusal to spend funds appropriated by Congress, the attempted intimidation of the press, the use of the White House itself as a base for espionage and sabotage directed against the political opposition—all signaled the extension of the imperial Presidency from foreign to domestic affairs.

An excerpt from the taped transcripts indicates how bewildered Nixon (New York Times, 1973: 85-86) was over the thirty-five-year sentence given to E. Howard Hunt by Judge Sirica in order to get him to talk. The other four plumbers received forty-year terms.

> You know they talk about a 35-year sentence, here is something to think about. There were no weapons! Right? There were no injuries! Right? There was no success! Why does that sort of thing happen? It's just ridiculous!

The break-in, after all, was an intelligence gathering maneuver, not much different from similar operations in other administrations. Evidence from the White House tapes, and a gamut of testimony before congressional inquirers indicates that Nixon and his aides saw many of these deeds, and especially the use of the FBI and Internal Revenue Service, as a prerogative of the President. Nixon knew that other presidents had bugged people, and that the practice was widespread. The soon-to-be-dethroned President didn't understand why everyone was so upset about an attempt to bug Democratic headquarters. In discussing the resultant investigation of the "buggers," and after being told by one of his aides that this was a larger inquiry than probed President Kennedy's assassination, Nixon (New York Times, 1973: 59) agreed that the whole thing was silly:

> Yes . . . Goldwater put it in context when he said, "Everybody bugs everybody else. You know that." It happens to be totally true. We were bugged in '68 on the plane and in '62 even for running for governor.

Theodore White (1975: 325) corroborates this view.

> Too many of the subordinate instruments of intelligence of the American government—the CIA, the FBI, the defense intelligence agencies—had crossed the threshold of law years before. They were there to be used. The clumsy break-in at Democratic headquarters in 1972 by Nixon men was technically criminal but of no uglier morality than the spying at Barry Goldwater's headquarters which Howard Hunt of the CIA had supervised for Lyndon Johnson in 1964. Their penchant for wire-tapping must certainly have been stimulated by the wire-tapping

authorized by Johnson against the Nixon campaign of 1968. Their
little early illegalities must have come naturally—and must have seemed
only a step beyond those of their predecessors.

Indeed, Nixon knew that former Attorney General Robert Kennedy
also bugged people when the occasion called for it. Later on in the
same conversation, Nixon commented: "Did your friends tell you
what Bobby did? . . . Johnson believed that Bobby bugged him."
So common was this practice that, in order to defend themselves
and show that bugging the opposition was not all that deviant, the
Nixon people considered publicizing Democratic buggings that
occurred prior to 1968. The following exchange took place on
February 28, 1973 (New York Times, 1973: 85) between President Nixon and White House Counsel John Dean.

Nixon: Yeah, Goldwater claims he was bugged.

Dean: That's right. Now I think that threats—

Nixon: Didn't you say that Johnson did bug Goldwater?

Dean: Well, I don't know if he bugged him.

Nixon: He did intelligence work?

Dean: He [with the FBI] did intelligence up one side and down the other.

Nixon's people took it for granted that this occurred. For example, in 1968 they employed electronic experts to sweep their
headquarters once a month for bugs, wiretaps, and listening devices. They knew about Johnson's famous "Five O'Clock Club,"
a group of innovative dirty tricksters who terrorized Goldwater's
campaign (White, 1975: 99). And they knew how Moira O'Connor,
a subordinate of well-known Democratic spy and trickster Dick
Tuck had "used her good looks and cover as a journalist to collect
juicy tid-bits for the Democrats" (Arizona Republic, June 24,
1972). It is reasonable to assume that Nixon was aware of the extensive behind-the-scenes political games that were played in order
to protect your position, and undermine the opposition's. This
awareness was again illustrated in a taped conversation with John
Dean on February 28, 1973. After observing that it was really silly

for the committee staff to work with Segretti in the first place, Nixon added (New York Times, 1973: 88):

> But nevertheless, what the hell did he do? . . . Shouldn't we be trying to get intelligence? Weren't they trying to get intelligence from us?

Dean's reply of "Absolutely," led to the following exchange:

Nixon: Don't you try to disrupt their meetings? Didn't they try to disrupt ours? . . . They threw rocks, ran demonstrations, shouted, cut the sound system, and let the tear gas in at night. What the hell is that all about? Did we do that?

Dean: McGovern had Dick Tuck on his payroll, and Dick Tuck was down in Texas when you were down at the Connally ranch and set up to do a prank down there. But it never came off.

Nixon: What did Segretti do that came off?

Dean: He did some humorous things. For example, there would be a fund-raising dinner, and he hired Wayne the Wizard to fly in from the Virgin Islands to perform a magic show. He sent invitations to all the black diplomats and sent limousines out to have them picked up, and they all showed up and they hadn't been invited. He had 400 pizzas sent to another—

Nixon: Sure! What the hell! Pranks! Tuck did those things in 1960, and all the rest.

These materials do not prove anything, but do indicate that President Nixon and his friends saw their tactics as normal under the circumstances. But they never envisioned the discrete events being put together "as the whole thing," as part of a long-term plan of lawlessness, or at least not as any less lawful than the activities of their predecessors. Indeed, subsequent revelations about the extensive use of the FBI by Presidents Johnson and Kennedy and the wiretapping of people like Martin Luther King suggest that Nixon was quite conservative in his assessment about how normal his actions were for Presidents. And they certainly didn't expect the events of Watergate to be treated as symptomatic of a "morality crisis." But this was how they were treated by journalists and some social scientists (cf. Lyman, 1975).

The general context of a more powerful presidency, and Nixon's interpretation of what that meant, were neglected in the news reports. This omission led newsworkers to look elsewhere for the significance of these events.

While neglecting the broader issue of history, reporters did link the Watergate break-in to other discoveries about the Nixon administration. This was done retrospectively, or by interpreting one event as though it were related to the others. In this way, a series of discrete events was seen as a process. The reinterpretation of these events as evidence of moral abandon gave the original break-in a different meaning, and in the process created the aftermath that has been referred to as the "fire storm." Indeed, the most significant result of all the news coverage was including a variety of angles under one heading—Watergate. For example, the Washington *Post* editorial of April 4, 1974, stated:

> As more and more allegations come tumbling out . . . it becomes increasingly difficult to keep track of that cluster of episodes and issues that are generally lumped under the heading of Watergate. The heart of the matter is all the more easily lost sight of when the argument turns on such questions as the precise role of this or that White House aide or former Cabinet member in the sleazier aspects of the campaign. . . . For all of these questions lead us away from the central fact, no longer susceptible to challenge: that both the integrity and the future quality of the political process in this country have been called profoundly into question by the behavior in the 1972 presidential campaign of that mysterious institution known cryptically as the Committee for the Re-Election of the President . . . we believe that the central point can be clearly perceived right now. It is that a group of people acting on behalf of, and indeed in the name of, the President of the United States, subverted the political process in this country in the last election in a way which has no parallel in any presidential election in this country that we have ever heard about.

Theodore White (1973: 367) cautioned against this unity. After detailing how many people worked for the Committee to Re-Elect the President, and that many members of these "teams" did not even know each other, he adds:

Each of these major personalities in the campaign of 1972 thus had his own role, his own field team, his own ambition. Later, when the mythology of Watergate reached full flower in 1973, the theory of the giant conspiracy, to suborn and undermine both justice and democratic tradition, was to conceive of all these operations as if some diabolical band of planners had contrived one master adventure. But the campaign of 1972 from the Republican side was more like the backfield of a football team with no quarterback and four footballs to run with—every ball carrier racing off on his own play—and the coach, who understood best what the campaign was all about, was preoccupied with action elsewhere.

The Watergate break-in, and its aftermath, were presented as a piece of a larger package. The *Post*'s editorial of August 29, 1972, criticized the amount, source, and use of Nixon's campaign funds. It concluded.

> The questions are so numerous and so grave, that nothing less than a full disclosure by the President of all the sources of his campaign funds and the appointment of a special investigatorial and prosecutorial team from outside the government would seem to be required to dispel the Republican-created sense that there is a great deal of dirty business in the effort to re-elect this particular President of the United States.

George McGovern (Knappman, 1973: 13) saw Watergate as a sign of the times. On September 16, 1972, he said:

> There has been a growing pattern of immorality associated with the Russian wheat deal, with the ITT case, with the handling of campaign funds, and now the latest revelation with regard to the invasion of the Democratic headquarters.

Such symbolic linkages of the break-in to the other events made the various agents appear to be co-conspirators, or teammates in a scheme to usurp proper conduct.

An associated image was the unscrupulous, reckless, and cunning character of the main participants. In the case of Nixon, this was easy, since his long-term relationship with the press had been one of the worst of any American president. Compared to President Kennedy, Nixon was a poor last when it came to press

relations. David Halberstam (1974) suggests that Kennedy's court-
ing of the press led them to not thoroughly scrutinize his administration (cf. Sorenson, 1965: 310-326). Kennedy was a popular
president, partly because he got along well with the press, but we
knew less about his government. Nixon did the opposite. We know
more about Nixon because he alienated the Washington press
corps. For one thing, he did not like their criticism, but more
importantly, he was annoyed when his accomplishments in envi-
ronmental restoration, revenue sharing, and foreign policy went
either unnoticed or were berated (cf. White, 1975). But a more
fundamental problem was that he felt that the press, and especially the networks, distorted what most people wanted. He felt
they spoke for themselves and for other small groups of intellectuals. White (1973: 330) observes,

> Within the new concentration of power, the significant heights of
> influence had been 'seized' by men of a world-view, and of a culture,
> entirely alien to his own. These were the adversary press. Its luminaries
> not only questioned his exercise of power. . . . They questioned his own
> understanding of America; they questioned not only his actions by the
> quality of his mind, and his honor as a man. It was a question of who
> was closest in contact with the mood of the American people—the
> President or his adversary press?

This mutual antagonism led him to have the fewest number of
press conferences—28 in his first term—of any full-term president
since Franklin Delano Roosevelt. This policy prevented reporters
from getting close to him and doing their work and, therefore,
stopped them from asking the questions about the issues and
problems they were interested in. It was easier for this President
to avoid arguments, and embarrassing questions. His first Vice
President, Spiro Agnew, once said, "I believe you should be able
to have a press conference without having reporters key in on
certain divisive issues" (Schlesinger, 1975: 226). Even more
infuriating for journalists was Nixon's use of the media. He held
more prime-time TV talks than any other president, and he cam-
paigned in 1972 mostly by a series of radio broadcasts. Thus,
Nixon and his closest aides believed that the journalism fraternity,
liberals, and intellectuals would use the Watergate break-in to get

him. In a conversation with John Dean on March 3, 1973, Nixon said (New York Times, 1973: 120):

> They are going to lie around and squeal. They are having a hard time now. They got the hell kicked out of them in the election. There is not a Watergate around in this town, not so much our opponents, even the media, but the basic thing is the establishment. The establishment is dying, and so they've got to show that despite the success we have had in foreign policy and in the election, they've got to show that it is just wrong just because of this. They are trying to use this as the whole thing.

Nixon was not the only person cast in an unflattering role. Throughout this media campaign to make sense out of what happened in the context of the dominant theme and angles noted above, the various characters were presented as either being uncontrolled or willing to let the ends justify the means. During an exchange on July 10, 1973, between John Mitchell and congressional interrogators, the former Attorney General claimed that he would have done anything to get Nixon re-elected. When asked by Senator Talmadge if he had "placed expediency of the next election" over the responsibility to "advise the President of the peril that surrounded him," Mitchell replied:

> Senators, I think you have put it exactly correct. In my mind, the re-election of Richard Nixon, compared with what was available on the other side, was so much more important that I put it in just that context.

This became another nail in the Nixon administration's coffin. But a careful reading of the entire Watergate episode reveals how widespread rule violations were: Many of the actors on both sides of this drama let the ends justify the means. The journalists who broke the original story, Carl Bernstein and Bob Woodward, illegally questioned a grand juror to get information for one of their reports. On another occasion, they blackmailed an FBI agent to have a report verified (Bernstein and Woodward, 1974). Even Judge Sirica used ends to justify means. Satisfied that the stonewalling defendants would crack under pressure, Sirica sentenced E. Howard Hunt to thirty-five years in prison, and the other four

defendants to forty-year terms. Judge Sirica defended this judgment (White, 1975: 204-205).

> I don't think the government wants a pound of flesh out of you. That
> is very little benefit to society . . . there will be a flurry of publicity as
> a result of your guilty pleas, naturally, but in a week or so it will be
> forgotten about. But, you see, I don't want it forgotten. So I have told
> your attorneys that the sentence that I will impose on you—and I am
> making no promise of leniencies . . . but *the sentence I will impose will
> depend primarily on whether or not you cooperate with the United
> States Senate.* . . . I fully expect you to cooperate absolutely, com-
> pletely and entirely with . . . that Senate committee [italics added].

As wiretapper G. Gordon Liddy (White, 1975: 341) understood
Sirica's logic: "John and I think alike. I mean that he believes
the end justifies the means." This does not mean that we should
not expect more of our elected officials, but it does suggest that
there is a great discrepancy between rules for governing situations
and the situations themselves. Thus, no one attacked Judge Sirica
for punishing the Watergate seven in order to make them talk; no
one suggested that he was invoking cruel and unusual punishment.
But the Los Angeles *Times* did attack Sirica on October 6, 1972
for issuing a gag rule:

> The order is a shocking abuse of judicial power, an obvious infringe-
> ment of constitutional rights. There simply is no evidence to support
> the premise of Judge Sirica that publicity makes impossible a fair trial.
> The whole history of judicial operation in an open and free society
> demonstrates the contrary, that the best assurance of a fair trial is
> freedom of information.

The news reports did not cause the burglary to happen and
did not cause other White House-related activities to occur. But
they did treat these activities as unique and did not seek to show
similarities with other administrations. In short, the knowledge
of widespread violation of a variety of constitutional rights by
federal agencies operating under the auspices of elected officials
did not lead to publication and persecution.

The number and nature of the Watergate reports, along with
the public support of these revelations, were part of the events

that led newsworkers to investigate further. When it became clear that presidential corruption and immorality was a public issue, congressional committees began mobilizing and acting. And they uncovered other abuses of authority. In this sense, Frank Mankiewicz (1975: 83) is correct in saying that the "news happened" due to the work of the Ervin Committee and the Joint Committee on Internal Revenue Taxation. But the massive publication and focus made this happen in a way that had never before occurred. Whether any recent administration could have survived such a barrage and scrutiny must remain an academic question since there is so little information about the internal workings, campaign tactics, etc. of past presidents compared with Richard Nixon. Even had biographers not been loyal, we still would know very little.

Had it not been for the tapes, Nixon's denial of wrongdoing would have stood. Stated differently, detailed information about the workings of the White House were the axe which Nixon's executioners wielded—not his deeds or those of his subordinates. One implication may be that future presidents, like so many corporations and organizations, will continue to shroud their affairs in secrecy. Like Eagleton, Nixon learned how bits and pieces of information can recast one's past and thereby change the future when viewed through the news perspective.

Summary and Conclusions: The Power of News

The way news transforms an event into a national story has been examined. The power of news angles, especially when used in conjunction with more general themes, served to emphasize certain points to the exclusion of others. Whether an event is seen as an isolated case, or as part of a broader trend that is characteristic of the "times" or the nation as a whole, makes the difference between a local and national story. This technique is fostered by, and perpetuates, the news perspective, a way of seeing events for practical purposes linked to the organizational, epistemological and technological aspects of all news, and especially TV news.

This process was illustrated with two major national stories, the Eagleton case and the Watergate events. Eagleton's demise as a vice presidential hopeful was a product of news reporting. It was not simply that the journalists revealed some things about Eagleton's past. The way these reports were constructed emphasized his shaky future—the dominant theme, in light of his "lies" to McGovern and the reluctance of his physicians to grant him a clean bill of mental health. Other crucial parts of Eagleton's biography were neglected. Once the relevant theme had been selected, his achievements, ideas about politics, and even the stamina which got him through the hectic "week that was" were either completely overlooked or were interpreted within the context of his shaky future, dishonesty, and uncertain health. The slow news week further complicated the Eagleton story. Many journalists picked up the theme, and assigned their reporters to further investigate the man from Missouri. The net affect was to promote one part of Eagleton as his substantial self, an image compatible with journalistic criteria of a major story. Thus, Eagleton became the national story for a week.

His decision to quit the Democratic ticket was prompted by a lot of editorial pressure on the Democrats. Commentators and editorial writers accepted the prior reports about Eagleton. They then evaluated these reified notions of his biography in making their unanimous pronouncement: guilty as presented.

This is not to say that Eagleton may not have been a suitable candidate. Close scrutiny of his voting record, understanding of foreign policy, and his political acumen at getting legislation passed may have all been relevant. Indeed, his honesty might have also been an issue, but his past was not examined to discover if, for example, he had taken bribes, served vested interests, seemed reckless as a Senator, and so forth. None of this was considered because it was not relevant in the context of the way Eagleton was viewed. Thus, the news perspective provided *the story of Eagleton* rather than the *man himself*; a theme survived independently of his life experience. The Missouri senator's demonstrated competence as a legislator was made small by the widespread editorial pronouncement that he could not prove he would be competent in the future. All that remained was to construct the evidence to make the theme come true, and make it seem as though it were based on sound investigation. On this basis, Eagleton became a liability for the Democratic Party; they could not survive the "harsh reality."

The last major story dealt with was the famous Watergate break-in. Two years of investigations and reports by journalists and congressional committees led to President Nixon's resignation and the jailing of most of his staff. Unlike other analysts who argued that Nixon's power and seclusion ultimately led to his fall from power, I suggested that his actual conduct, like that of his predecessors, was of secondary importance compared to the massive publication and treatment of these events by news agents. Divorcing the events of Watergate from the historical context of a more powerful presidency painted Nixon as far more reckless than his predecessors. Another important context overlooked in the news presentations was the routine use of wiretaps and bugs in containing one's enemies. Thus, while the break-in *may* have been unique in presidential politics, bugging was not. Excluding the Watergate events from these contexts distorted their nature. Journalists were inclined to treat the break-in and other actions uncovered by their investigations as part of the same corrupt process. Once established, the theme of official corruption was told in many ways. The power of the news perspective led journalists to decontextualize events from the meaningful context of those who carried them out, in order to more smoothly tell a story. The net effect was to greatly exaggerate the crimes of Nixon while downplaying the questionable, but still routine, practices of other administrations and the negotiated and conflictful nature of everyday political life. Thus, the journalists, judge, and others involved in punishing Nixon and his aides for permitting ends to justify means had to resort to similar devices in bringing them to justice.

Analysis of the Eagleton and Watergate stories suggested that the practical circumstances of news production has led to viewing the world through a perspective which has consequences for the events that are featured by the stories, and for the viewers that learn from them. News routines and recipes are inextricably enmeshed in the guiding principle of doing *something* about an event that can be worked into a story. Pursuing events from a theme or angle independently of the event may provide good news, but incomplete understanding.

Setting forth the role of the news perspective and its role in shaping news events is crucial to understanding the nature of social issues, but it is not enough. We must go beyond merely demonstrating that the news does have its own perspective, to probe how this framework works, including its logic and assumptions about objectivity. This is essential is we are to improve journalistic procedures and become better informed news watchers.

Chapter 7

RETHINKING TV NEWS

The central thesis of this book is that events become news when transformed by the news perspective, and not because of their objective characteristics. A related point is that news practices can significantly alter one event by either predefining what is most important about it or by retrospectively connecting it to other events.

The way newsworkers look at the world was shown to be influenced by commercialism, political influence, technology, and scheduling demands. These concerns become *problems* which must be solved if news is to be presented in a concise and entertaining way. The *solution* is what I have termed the *news perspective, or the view that for practical purposes, events can and should be summarily presented as a narrative account with a beginning, middle, and end.* It must be emphasized that, within the various news organizations I have studied, the reliance on and use of this perspective is morally sanctioned in the form of job security, collegial praise, and journalistic awards. Thus, organization has prompted practices which obfuscate the events-presented-as-news for practical reasons. Rules of thumb, editing techniques, marketing research, use of themes and angles, and even writing a story to fit with another to make the "show flow," has become the rational way to change the world in order to present it as news.

This is the kind of news millions of people receive each night, and this is why I have argued throughout these chapters that the news process is itself a medium through which the world is viewed, selected, and then presented. It is the scene for significant events. My observations led me to the conclusion that *television news is most accurately conceived as a medium for presenting useful reports (e.g., organizational, personal, and political) as though they were derived for their truth, objectivity and adequacy.* The overriding practical commitments of local TV news have been substituted for more objective reports about social life.

The place of TV news in our everyday lives demands that everyone know how to watch it. This is necessary because our pictures of reality are distorted by the work which transforms events into news stories. We must realize that many events-presented-as-news are irremediably influenced by these prior commitments. A first step toward understanding our lives and knowing what is going on in our world is to become aware of the news process. We must see how newswork becomes a medium for journalists' images about the world. This has been one purpose of this book. Another purpose is to offer an alternative way to report and watch the news.

Two considerations are particularly important in understanding and then improving the news process. The first is the journalists' view of objectivity; the second is the way all news—and especially TV news—decontextualizes an event by presenting it as a news story. Paying some attention to each of these commonly accepted features of TV news illuminates a path through the unique bias of the news perspective.

Objectivity and TV News

Journalists see objectivity in practical terms. Work routines, along with commonsense beliefs which equate objectivity with fairness, lead to the acceptance of less than systematic ways to reduce bias. Newsworkers recognize various ways that a report can be misconstrued, including making mistakes, getting the facts wrong, and misinterpreting what someone said. The people

I studied often blamed the work schedule for mistakes. However, not having enough time to check things out or making a mistake in what was heard or filmed are not regarded by newsworkers as forms of bias.

There are two types of bias which journalists acknowledge might influence their work: personal values or preferences, and ideological commitments. While most reporters and cameramen deny "being biased," colleagues assess objectivity by noting the kinds of stories which are done and the way certain subjects are treated. The cameramen who were also reserve police officers illustrate this point. The likelihood that they would be involved with police stories, and the generally favorable reading they gave the police indicated to most of their colleagues that they were biased.

From the workers' perspective, inferior work may be due to inexperience, carelessness, or bias. But it is assumed that once a reporter or cameraman has some experience the quality of his work will meet certain professional standards. One way to be "professional" is by giving evidence that some research has been done, and that all sides of an issue (usually two) are given. This procedure of "getting the facts" within the time allowed, and then, if appropriate, eliciting divergent views from spokespersons, are the essentials of good work. If possible, quotes are preferred, since this not only "put the interviewee in the picture," but also reduces the likelihood that a report might be challended as "unfair."

According to this view, all events are essentially the same; they are objects which can be studied independently of the interpretations or meanings and the processes which create them. A fire and a city council meeting can be described, filmed, and recorded in much the same way. I will show in a moment that this view of objectivity leads journalists to conveive of events in terms of who, what, where, and when. This orientation enables journalists to decide on the "facts," although their version of facts is always a practical matter. For example, reporters can use quotations as facts to get at the truth. If a story is opinionated, "all the facts" can be obtained by getting the "other side" and letting both parties be quoted. If there is some dispute about the "facts," then agreement among reporters is the test of truth. Generally speaking, the more reporters agree, the more confidence they have in their reports. From this perspective, journalists use methods of investigation and presentation, but the people involved in the events to be reported do not; they are objects which do certain objective deeds with objective consequences. The journalist simply has to be around to pick up the pieces and put them together. The way all segments are joined to make a story is presumed to be due to a reenactment of history; the facts speak for themselves, although occasionally requiring some interpretation to put them in their proper perspective. This theory of events proclaims that the only indeterminate feature in understanding events is the reporter's skill, experience, and control of bias.

Reporters currently use procedures which embrace the view of objectivity just presented. They act as though the most important biases can be reduced by being fair and acting in good faith. In doing so, they overlook the bias of the news perspective. The impact of work routines and orientation on the events they report as news stories is assumed to be nil. But, as noted previously, and as the Eagleton and Watergate stories illustrated, asking questions, eliciting information, and reconstructing a series of events requires a general focus to begin with. Reporters, scientists, and laymen never start an inquiry with the "facts," since even the recognition of a "fact" requires a great deal of prior knowledge and theory about a particular phenomenon. Newsworkers, like scientists and laymen, begin their quest for "facts" with a storehouse of common sense, and, as with most other specialists, their training, experience, and purpose lead them to further refine a way of seeing and knowing the world. I have referred to this orientation as a perspective.

Newsworkers, physicians, teachers, engineers, attorneys, and other practitioners have unique organizing principles; what one sees as important is irrelevant to another. And just as a physician cannot cure our physical ills without looking at the body in a peculiar way, newsworkers cannot perform their tasks without adopting a special outlook. While physicians may look for blood pressure, swelling of lymph nodes, and body temperature, journalists look for angles, interest, and entertainment value. To carry the analogy a bit further, physicians see what their instruments and theories of the body permit. Similarly, news agents have evolved theories of newscasts involving commercialism, entertainment, story lines, and narrative form. This perspective leads these practitioners to select and view events in peculiar ways.

This orientation is a more troublesome bias than values and ideology because fellow journalists, like most of the audience, take the perspective for granted; it is unchallenged because it is not seen as a source of distortion. Most importantly, there can be no effective check on the bias of this perspective unless it is articulated and shown to be operative. Thus, reporters can agree about the "facts" but still distort an event by pursuing one angle and thereby removing the event from the context in which it occurred, in which it would be more fully understood. Some social scientists have duplicated this error in investigating the news process (Danzger, 1975: 582).

> Inaccuracies which might occur in a given report if observed only by a single individual are corrected by others also observing the phenomenon. . . . The reporters often exchange information with each other and in the process, reports become more accurate.

While it is important that a report be *accurate,* it is far more important that a report be *relevant* to the event it represents.

The news perspective which informs current reporting practices satisfies organizational and other practical criteria, but, for the most part, it does not permit disclosures of relevant aspects of events. Efforts to use this knowledge are not likely to succeed, since only a portion of the event has been selected for presentation. For example, driving Nixon from the White House had little to do with increasing presidential power, widespread reliance on nonelected bureaucrats, campaign contributions by vested interests, coverups, or running government through media presentations and public relations techniques. These features of our government were present before Nixon took office, and they remain. Focusing on the "facts" of the break-in, the "facts" of the obstruction of justice, and the like made them look like the most important aspects of Nixon's, or any other, administration. The emphasis on the man rather than the organization and routines of modern government did not serve the public interest; indeed, many people still think that the Nixon bunch was substantially different from the norm. But the "fact" that it has not been much different for the past three administrations was not made clear. Clarifying why certain facts are selected is essential to making reports accurate, relevant, and socially useful.

News practices will provide the public with useful information when another view of objectivity is adopted. As long as journalists act as though the important aspects of an event are obvious and meaningful independently of the situation or of the interests of the reporter, then news reports will contribute little to our understanding of social life. Before reports can be useful, they must be complete; they must grasp all relevant aspects of an event.

The first step toward better news is the recognition of the vast difference between social phenomena and the physical world. The latter is easier to treat as an object because it is less subject to variation. But social phenomena are influenced—and actually constituted—by cultural and social meanings. Unlike physical things, human events cannot be divorced from the interpretive processes that create them. Whereas physical events are not subject to their own meanings—but only to the observer's—social situations are defined and interpreted by the people directly involved, and the observer-journalist. This may be stated as a general principle: *Events are more difficult to understand—and less object-like—if they are susceptible to ambiguity of meaning and interpretation.* In specific terms, this distinction suggests that more people agree what fire is than what morality is. And this difference must be acknowledged before adopting particular methods. With social phenomena, we must realize that the meanings and context of an act need to be clarified before we say what it is and what the facts are. (Indeed, journalists are very concerned about their work being taken out of context.) Any effort to study these topics in the same way, or cover them as news items using the same techniques, would be doomed to irrelevance. A "fire problem" can be communicated with film of a blazing building, but does anyone think the same process can be applied to a "moral problem?" There would be little disagreement about the former, but great disagreement about the latter.

And this is the dilemma. Fire is part of our shared cultural wisdom and daily experience; we may not be able to explain it, but we recognize it when we see it. This clarity is much less true of morality. Anyone with common sense would not think of using the same technique to obtain valid information on these matters. Unfortunately, TV news personnel have done precisely this. The same general procedure is used in covering an interview with the mayor as is used in covering a fire; both are treated as objects in order to answer the central questions of who, what, where, and when. This is what must be changed if TV news is going to improve and give us more useful information.

Journalistic claims to objectivity can be strengthened by considering all potential sources of bias, including the impact of the news process itself. *By news process I mean the organized and routine assumptions and procedures which contribute to the definition, selection, coverage, and presentation of events-as-news.* Journalists and news watchers must not only be concerned with unravelling the complexities of the event(s) in question, but also with the impact of "news coverage" on the people and situations. We have already seen in previous chapters how commercialism, scheduling, technology and entertainment considerations influence newswork by promoting the news perspective. What remains to be done, however, is to more fully describe how these practices may remove an event from the context in which it occurs, in order to present it as news.

News Events in Context

Journalists traditionally approach a potential story by asking who, what, where, when, why. Answers to these questions are presumed to provide the relevant facts to be investigated, though in practice the question of "why" is addressed by answering the first four queries. Accordingly, this section turns the first four journalistic questions on the news process itself in order to clarify "why" news is the way it is. One intent is to show how the news process contributes to *decontextualizing,* or removing an event from the context in which it occurs in order to *recontextualize* it within news formats. Another reason for focusing on who, what, where, and when of news reports is to show how news watchers can approach TV's versions of the day's significant events in a more critical manner. This orientation enjoins viewers to "watch defensively," as it provides ways of making sense out of news reports. At the same time, however, a viewer must draw on personal knowledge about the world in order to consider optional ways of treating a particular subject. But I think the first step is to be aware that news is reported from definite, but limited, perspectives.

WHO

News practices promote the coverage of certain persons, organizations, and institutions. And few of these media targets appear against their will, which suggests that they are interested in receiving news coverage. As I have already shown, most of this coverage can be regarded as favorable toward them. Their purposes, and the cooperation of TV news in fulfilling them, are part of the context of news reports. This is why it is important to focus on "who" is involved in a story and "who" it is about. Taking note of the participants, their views, and then noting which relevant parties are omitted from the presentation is a first step toward making explicit the implicit links between news sources, publicity, and the active involvement of news messages in the events that are reported. One example is news coverage about skid row life. Who speaks: skid row ministers or the other residents? If only the former, then why not the latter? I have yet to see a report on skid row life which systematically examines the perspective of those who live there. Rather, the residents are usually viewed as victims or failures who are looking for handouts, while mission ministers and other caretakers are shown as unselfish people who continue to follow their calling despite its hopelessness. This is at least partly due to the reporter's commonsense thinking about skid rowers and how they got there, and it is a feature of the news perspective.

In addition to "who" is involved, one must also be aware of the immediate and practical interests of the interviewees. This question should be emphasized in those cases where the speaker appears to be disinterested since we know that *all* human communication is interested. Indeed, one is well advised to be suspicious of those persons who strive to appear disinterested. While this contrived lack of interest may seem to be more "objective," it has little basis in reality in front of a mass audience. Paradoxically, then, while all human communication is informed by various interests, public appearances may be cast as less interested and involved—and are therefore more liable to suspicion than obviously interested parties, whose motives do not need to be sought.

The importance of who is involved in a report is illustrated by news reports and editorials in 1974-1975 that Phoenix, Arizona, was experiencing a crime wave. This view was partly based on FBI Uniform Crime Reports showing that crime had increased in Phoenix, to the point where it had the top crime ranking for all U.S. cities. The effects of changes in crime classification and crime reporting on this increase were never examined. I suggested the relevance of new reporting procedures during a conversation with a journalist who was developing a series on the crime and justice problem. He replied, "Of course there has been a change in crime categories, but there is still a crime wave."

The acceptance of the FBI report as valid led to the cries for more "law and order" and "mandatory sentencing," and provided more material for irresponsible editors to blame it all on our "permissive society." The main source for most of the information was the Chief of Police, who, like his colleagues in other cities, felt the tide of crime could be turned by an investment of more money. But reporters did not try to check out whether crime had increased. Rather than talking to the officers on the street about their perceptions of the avowed increase in crime, the official spokespersons were taken at their word.

My students and I conducted several interviews with police officers in the metropolitan area about their views of crime. We found that a few felt crime had increased in the areas where they worked, others felt it had stayed about the same or had increased, and still others had not thought much about it. One even said that he first learned about the "crime wave" from the news media! If reporters had considered talking to officers on the "beat," they might have discovered that the increase in crime was a statistical artifact, and that there were practical reasons for adjusting the rates. One officer explained how a particular crime rate had been constructed.

> It fluctuates. I have seen it take a turn about twice. Before, everything was a burglary. If the door was open and it looked like somebody got in, that was a burglary. . . . Okay, our burglary rate was high, it wasn't looking good, so they came out and said anything that is not definitely

a burglary, with grand or petty theft or other felony, where we can actually show intent without question, then make it malicious mischief. That was in 1971 and carried through '72. . . . Because of executive order we were writing off burglaries as malicious mischief because there was nothing taken. Then there was another turnaround. And now we're obligated to report everything where entry is made as a burglary. . . . Consequently our burglary rate has gone up.

This officer, and several of his colleagues, had a different assessment of the "crime wave" scare than did their superiors, but their view was overlooked by those newspaper and television reporters assigned to cover the "crime news." Also overlooked was any assessment of the "practical consequences" of such crime-wave scare tactics, such as, for example, how they related to a fifty-four percent increase of police manpower between 1969-1974.

Other examples of the impact certain spokespersons can have on resulting news reports are not hard to find. The majority of reports about the Vietnam war were derived from military spokesmen. This was especially true before 1968 and the eye-opening Tet offensive. The success of the Viet Cong attacks, and their obvious strength, made short shrift of the media reports that the enemy was being worn down. Correspondents cannot be expected to know all the answers, but they can be expected to know the right questions—especially, who is giving the information, and whether they have a vested interest in what is made public.

There are always others to ask, including troops in the field or intelligence personnel. An example of the latter is Sam Adams (1975), who worked for the CIA during the period preceeding the Tet offensive which took 6,000 American lives. Adams was in charge of estimating the Viet Cong's strength, which his data revealed as twice as great as the Pentagon and State Department acknowledged. But his request for updating the figures was sent through so many channels that it took the Tet offensive to indicate how far off the military spokesmen had been. This is not just hindsight.

We have known for years that official reports are usually self-serving, which indicates that official spokesmen, such as press secretaries, should never be taken at their word insofar as "all the truth" is desired. This is as true of presidents as it is of mayors, school superintendents, police chiefs, and university administrators. Who is asked for information, and who is involved in a story, are central dimensions of the news context. Some people, like mayors, are routinely relied on by reporters for statements because they are public officials. But we, as viewers or listeners, should never assume that they know more about many facets of decision-making than their secretaries or other assistants.

The impact of focusing on a particular person or creating a certain impression of someone helps shape the meaning of the news report. The adventures of Patty Hearst in 1974-1975 illustrate this point. The kidnapping of Ms. Hearst by the Symbionese Liberation Army (SLA) and her subsequent participation in their robbery and murder schemes made the headlines for many months. The best examples of the news perspective appeared following her capture, when many people's opinions were solicited for judicial and news purposes regarding her character and stability. Among the people interviewed were her parents, attorneys, psychiatrists, FBI and police officials, childhood friends, former schoolmates, sociologists, psychologists, counselors, and reporters.

A brief contrast with news reports of other criminals shows Patty Hearst to be unique. "Typical" crimes are presumed to be committed by "typical" criminals. Covering their story amounts to stating "facts": who, what, where, and when. Most importantly, the accused is presented as the kind of person who does these things. Before a TV reporter tells the story, he may interview a police spokesman, but will almost never talk with the suspect's friends, former teachers, childhood friends, psychologists, etc. Procedures for getting out the news forbid "making a big deal" out of any armed robbery. The impression the media therefore give is that most crime stories are simpler than Patty Hearst's. That news reports can treat crimes in such different ways has less to do with the nature of the Hearst offense compared to "typical" crimes, than with journalistic practices. Thus, "who" is involved in a report often affects and is affected by the news perspective.

WHAT

Clarifying "what" journalists report adds more to our understanding of the relationship between newswork and news reports.

"What" gets reported is often as practical a matter as "who" is consulted, interviewed, and shown; the two are necessarily related. If a police chief is asked for his assessment of crime, he is likely to say it is increasing, but can be held in check with more money for equipment and manpower. If a presidential press secretary is asked if the commander in chief is really a crook, he is likely to say no. And generals will say wars are being won even if they are being lost. Each has a stake in the public acceptance of their statements, which can be viewed as efforts to promote a particular focus.

The pertinence of "what" for defensive viewing is more evident if it is recalled that one's interest, orientation, and practical purpose establish the relevance in a situation. Indeed, articulating "what" an event is about can establish that definition as the essence or nature of the event. For the journalists working on a story, and for the viewer watching the report, this means that any claim of "facts" or "truth" must be questioned until the context of the message, questions, answers, and evidence have been assessed.

The first step is to realize that almost anything could be said about any event, and then inquire why one point or perspective is emphasized and not others. TV coverage of crime and social problems illustrates the arbitrary way in which some events are reported. The circumstances, motives, and contingencies involved in most crimes are not focused on or treated as problematic. Reporters, police officials, and many viewers assume that most criminal acts occur within, and because of, one's moral and economic environment. From this perspective, it makes sense when poor and minority group people commit crimes, and there is little need for elaboration. Few police officials, and fewer reporters, question their understanding of the situation, or even whether mitigating circumstances should be considered. In short, "what" happened is presented within a context of taken-for-granted "knowledge" about the way the world works—even though this "knowledge" may in fact be incomplete, distorted, and dissonant with the way the accused see and feel their acts.

But the situation is different when, for instance, wealthy suspects like Patty Hearst are accused of robbing a bank, or health insurance officials are suspected of fraud. Now it is no longer so obvious what happened, or what should be done; things become more complex. As a state official said when I asked if he suspected that fraudulent practices sent an insurance company into receivership, "No, no, of course not." However, minutes later, he explained that part of the problem was due to "a constant juggling of the books in order to stay in business," a practice that, in his words, "eventually caught up with them." My question seemed strange to this bureaucrat because "what" happened, from his perspective, was poor management and nothing else.

As we saw with Patty Hearst, things get more complicated; different questions need be asked in order to obtain justice, and many of these questions will be raised by reporters in an attempt to resolve the crisis, to "get to the bottom" of the Hearst case, an abyss apparently far more complicated than "what" everyone knows to be true of most "small-time criminals."

Such practices are seldom recognized for their distorting capacity. Thus, viewers must learn to watch defensively and scrutinize what they assume reporters and others know about a situation. Even though a viewer may not know as much as the person "on the scene," he or she may raise key questions about any report. For example, it is not just a matter of having the proper facts. It is a matter of perspective. When more of our information is derived from news, we must appreciate the contribution of the news perspective to assessments of "what" is going on.

Routine news procedures do not permit new insights into how the social world works. Rather, the employment of angles enables journalists to do their work, and tell their stories according to unstated theories and beliefs. Their work thus consists less of sorting out explanations and reasons than it does in obtaining evidence to fit preconceived notions. In rare instances where persons accused of crimes are allowed to speak for themselves, their stories are told from a "human interest" point of view. An example would be an account of a convict's "reform" and his desire to help others avoid his own mistakes. The circumstances of his original crime may be told, if not reconstructed, to show that he was really not all that guilty in the first place, but was a victim of circumstance. However, checking the news accounts of these stories as originally presented at the time of the crime

will reveal that these extenuating circumstances were not mentioned; at news time the stories were cut-and-dried.

News reports of the attempt by Sara Moore to kill President
Ford illustrate the power of perspective and taken-for-granted
understandings about the causes of deviance and order. On Monday, September 22, 1975, Sara Moore fired a shot at President
Ford as he emerged from the St. Francis Hotel in San Francisco.
The explanation for her act has been shrouded in various terms
by the major media. *Time's* (October 6, 1975) extended coverage
of the event illustrates the news perspective's easy use of unex-
amined cliches and theories. After noting how violence-prone
American society is, *Time* asks its four and one-half million
readers, "Is it [American society] so sick that it spawns and
encourages the lethal fantasies of its alienated mental misfits?"
(p. 6) And then, "Somebody, if not all Americans must bear the
blame." The problem, according to the "sick society" theme, is
that

> There seems no practical way for a free country to go about deliber-
> ately reducing the chances of producing lonely, disoriented individuals
> who lash out at a President to fulfill some antisocial personal need. . . .
> Inevitably the question arises: Is there something wrong with American
> society? Why does America seem to have so many kooks willing to kill
> to exorcise some private demon? (p. 8)

Sara Moore's act was thereby explained as the product of a "sick
society" which produces more than its share of "kooks." According to this view, although she had no plausible reason for taking
a shot at Ford, *Time* feels it has to present a rational strategy.

Sara Moore's association with a variety of radical groups led to
her acting as a messenger between Randolph Hearst and someone
believed to have contact with kidnappers of Hearst's daughter
Patty. This role attracted the attention of the FBI, who hired
Moore to inform on several radical groups. However, her contact
with these circles and her personal involvements led her to adopt
the Marxist position she had originally been hired to help suppress.
When she told her newfound "friends" about her role as an informant they wanted nothing to do with her. In her words, "I
was afraid of [the] group, and I was afraid of the bureau if they

found out I told." Finally, the FBI dropped her as an informant, although she continued to work with local police officials. She schemed to kill Ford in order to convince the radicals that she was loyal and could be trusted. After buying a gun from an officer in the John Birch Society, whom she had tried to "set up" for illegal gun sales only days before, and hinting to police officials that she was going to "test the system," Sara Moore waited for the President across the street from the St. Francis Hotel. She was standing next to another "social misfit," Oliver Sipple.

Sipple, the man who deflected Moore's gun, was not reliable, stable, or disciplined. Physically and psychologically impaired by a nightmarish experience in Vietnam, Sipple was unable to work or to tolerate many of the pressures of daily life. In his words, "I'd be fine for awhile, then someone might say something to me and boom." Even though he had no electronic gear, expert training, or keen reflexes, he was the one who foiled Moore's plan.

It is plain that several aspects of the Ford assassination attempt were reported from a unique perspective. "What" was said was less a feature of the events and their interrelationship than it was a series of separate stories which were written from different, but predefined angles. Sara Moore was treated as a reject and her problematic identity and misplaced sense of loyalty were presented as evidence of a deranged mind, the product of a "sick society." Moore's worries about her nine-year-old son getting home from school were mentioned but not stressed, since this would have upset the story line about her "kookiness." Sipple was apparently not as sick, although he admitted having trouble negotiating the demands of everyday life. Thus, we were left with the view that those who commit certain crimes are fundamentally different from those who prevent them—and explanations of what happened were more informed by news practices than by any real understanding of the complex events.

The power of this perspective can also be seen in what is presented as normal or official acts. This is especially true of press conferences. Examining the impact of news coverage on these orchestrated events further clarifies what is reported.

The avowed purpose of a press conference may be to "speak out" on an important issue, but the underlying purpose is often to get public exposure. This becomes easier to understand if it is remembered that few people appear on television news against their will. Unless these self-serving interests are clarified, and the implicit use of TV news is made explicit, an important part of the message may be lost. This is especially true of politicians who desire recognition and will discuss a variety of issues in front of cameras in order to get it. TV journalists must present the various reasons for televising some stories, or else the public will be used by those seeking to generate publicity. Contrary to current practices, newsworkers might even investigate who the message is intended for and what purpose it is to serve. If the habitually self-serving users of the press are aware that this analysis will precede or follow most TV news reports, they will be more reluctant to equate their own interests with news, and the audience will be warned to consider the context of the message. At least, TV news viewers should be made aware that such practices routinely occur. When this is not done, newsworkers unwittingly permit a few people to manipulate the public awareness—successfully or not.

An example will illustrate the self-serving use by outsiders of media personnel. The failure of the County Attorney in Phoenix, Arizona, to prosecute a man charged with land fraud provided an occasion for a powerful group of business leaders to attack him. This group, called the "Phoenix 40," used press conferences to attack the County Attorney's competence, allegedly in the public interest. But their messages were not aimed at the public as much as they were directed toward influentials and other media in order to present the charge as a public issue. The business leaders understood that news coverage is tantamount to significance and importance; the greater the TV coverage, the more significant an event. Charges by the "Phoenix 40" were carried in all the print and electronic media, which were thus manipulated by members of this "concerned" group. Press conferences were an obvious way they could turn a personal disagreement into a media event which dominated the Phoenix news for nearly two weeks. The County Attorney was forced to answer the charges and repel his attackers through press conferences of his own, in which he tried to substantiate a claim that the "Phoenix 40" was out to get him because he had refused to play ball with their economic and political interests.

In overlooking the interests and motivations behind such charges, the news outlets were masking an important part of the message. For example, not one news story questioned whether the Phoenix 40's claim to represent the public interest was valid. The result was that an elected official's problems and competence became the issue, to the point where one reporter noted that the Attorney couldn't do a good job now because he was always fending off criticism.

The journalists' acceptance of a powerful group's definition of "what" was going on made them an accessory to the political assassination which resulted. Telling both sides of the story amounted to really telling only one: The Phoenix 40's charges were constantly dealt with and were legitimated as newsworthy concerns. The story could have been different if Phoenix journalists had examined and presented the more obvious political involvements, and their impact on what was presented as news. The charges and rebuttals could have been clarified by placing them in the context of the news process. In this case then, the news did not merely report what was happening; the news *was* what was happening; journalists were participants and not merely observers.

These comments about "what" is reported can also be seen in the routine use of angles, where messages and definitions are often so subtle that they require a trained eye and ear to pick them out. My earlier discussion of the Eagleton story illustrated one way this was done. The major focus of all the news reporters was on Eagleton's history of mental illness and his "lack of candor" in not telling McGovern about his past. These were the recurring angles used in presenting the overriding theme that he was unfit for the vice presidency. Famous network reporters questioned him about how he felt he could campaign for vice president when reports about his mental health dominated the news, and when he had to constantly react to these charges. Other reporters focused on the "fact" that his physicians could not guarantee that he would never have a recurrence of "nervous exhaustion" or that he was "cured."

Such questions would not have been asked if the journalists had known anything about mental illness; they would have been aware that it is not like a physical disorder, but is a condition prescribed by one's intimates if they perceive a change in behavior. But the emphasis was not on trying to understand the complexities and vastly changing notions of mental health. Nor was it on the great disagreements between physicians, psychiatrists, and social scientists over what constitutes mental illness, disagreements which are seldom found with physical illness. The journalists' predefinition of the Eagleton case led them away from these questions to the "facts" noted above: He had lied and he could not prove he was well. What they told about Eagleton, his past, present, and future, could not be separated from their problem of getting a big story during a slow news period, staying on top of a "breaking story," and the other practical problems of news noted throughout this book. The resulting stories were not merely "one-sided" and "oversimplifications," they fundamentally distorted Eagleton's situation. But it was news and it was easy to encapsulate. In brief, what is said cannot be distinguished from circumstances which engulf current news practices.

The importance of the news context can also be seen in reports about political contests. Television journalists' beliefs that their audience is unintelligent and desires to be entertained lead them to present news accounts which are brief and visual. No complex discussion is the general rule of television news. This leads journalists to look upon presidential contests as "horse races." Candidates are grouped according to their stands on major issues, and any differences are encapsulated by themes which might be helpful to some, and epitaphs to others. The "underdog" illustrates the former, while "politician of the past" or the "old warhorse" illustrates the latter. Underdogs are valued in American life; one who comes from behind and against great odds has public appeal. By the same token, the "politician of the past" is a way of saying something about what a person stands for, what his loyalties and interest are, and what kind of ideas he might have. These themes have been used in several presidential campaigns (e.g., 1968, 1972, 1976) to enable journalists to define what someone stands for and how he relates to the other candidates. All that remains for extended coverage of say, the "underdog" is to introduce the evening's news coverage with how much better he is doing, and then show one minute of film of the candidate walking among the people or talking informally with advisers. This is how presidential politics have been covered and this is *what* has been presented. The news context can also be understood by examining "where" news reports are learned about, "when" they occur and how long they last.

WHERE

Who is involved in a story, and what is reported are influenced by "where" the story is learned about. I showed in Chapter 3 that different news sources produce different stories. Police radio monitors, for example, provide crime news involving street crimes which frequently involve lower-class and minority group youth. But the story of crime is incomplete if it is only learned about from these sources. The image is presented, albeit unintentionally, that certain kinds of crime are not only committed by certain groups of people, but that this is what the crime problem is about. White-collar crime and corporate rip-offs are not presented via police monitors, even though more money is involved than in dozens of $25-$100 robberies. Thus, the Phoenix media were reluctant to disclose that one of the area's largest banks was being investigated for passing illegal securities. If bank officials *are* eventually indicted, they will be interviewed in their plush offices. In all likelihood we will never see film of them being "drug off" by police officers, handcuffed, dishevelled, and looking ashamed. This is how most TV film reports of suspects look. The key differences are the sources of information and the meaning attached to them.

Sources lend credibility to an event as they continue to focus on it. Patty Hearst was news because of who she is, but where the information came from, and the reporters' preoccupation with "getting the story" contributed to the event. The complexities of the case were magnified by the quest for more information, different interpretations, and finally, by efforts to sort out all the complexities themselves, created and compounded by the actual news process.

This point is more evident when the Hearst case is compared to other crimes, as most crimes are believed to not be mysterious or complex, but are rather seen as cut-and-dried. Apparently, reporters believe that someone does not engage in soul-searching or weigh alternatives before, say, robbing a bank or a convenient store. Or they believe that the influence of one's friends, the reaching for "rep," and a moral commitment to "keep one's word" are not involved in many criminal acts. Should this information become available and scrutinized with the same thoroughness as the Hearst material received, fewer crimes would be cut-and-dried, and the guilt of innocence of the persons involved would be more problematic. Of course, this is not done, mainly because police officials, journalists, and others in our society believe that the cases are substantially different: Hearst needs explaining, but the others are "obvious." From this perspective, there is little to tell about most criminals, but a lot to tell about Ms. Hearst. Most importantly, this presumption encourages "digging" in one case, but not in the other; and in the process one story becomes more difficult, while "normal crimes" are accounted for through common sense.

This difference will be reflected in the kinds of news sources drawn on, that become available in a given case. Many reports about "spectacular" crimes will come from "leaks." This source is, for the most part, unavailable to tell "typical criminal" stories. To be leaked about is to deserve an explanation. So there are seldom leaks about "small-time" criminals; being small-time implies that the authorities, then the journalists, and finally the public believe that their story is already known: for example, someone wanted money and robbed a store and he should be punished. There is no commiseration, little second-guessing, and seldom a hint of injustice in such reports. These cases, and their moral implications, are cut-and-dried. Not so with Patty Hearst. Many column inches and hours of news time were given to her adventures, motivation, the "turning point," and even to questions about her guilt. Why is this not true of other criminals? Because where the story is learned about is tied to who will be involved and what will be said. And both are central to current news practices.

The significance of where the story is learned about can be seen in press releases, the dominant news source for local stations. Press releases are the main news outlet for institutions and organizations. Each message is planned in order to favorably promote some aspect of the organization. These "handouts" could be regarded as advertisements, but it is their "timeliness" which qualifies them as news in the eyes of local stations. Nevertheless, presenting events to the news stations is intended to serve the interests of those in charge by using the audience. For example, school superintendents want parents to see and hear that children are receiving an adequate education. The viewers are a convenience, but from the perspective of a school superintendent, a necessary one, and one which causes most school superintendents to refrain from reporting the failings of the school, or its problems. In Chapter 3, I described one school official's reluctance to have a local station pursue an investigative report on violence in a high school. This man sought to take advantage of the role the media play in defining what is important and worthy of attention by encouraging the station not to broadcast a story detrimental to him. Taking advantage of the media is as likely for minority groups seeking redress for grievances as it was for pompous senators during the Watergate hearings. Moral statements, and even quotations from the Bible, enabled these national officials to present a manipulated TV image of congressmen at work. To cover these events without emphasizing the significance of the news coverage to what is presented, gives the false impression that the media are merely reporting and not constructing the event they report.

WHEN

What is said about an event, and where it is derived, are closely related to "when" the event is learned about. I stressed in Chapter 3 that television news meets a tight schedule, and this promotes reliance on certain news sources, including press releases. But the kind of news that is presented also depends on when stories get selected. A few examples will clarify this point.

Police radio monitors provide certain kinds of events which are presented as crime news. These events are not covered merely on the basis of a "spectacular crime," or anything of the sort, but are largely contingent on practical matters like the amount of time that needs to be filled in an upcoming newscast. Newsworkers assume that the amount of news varies by time of day, day of week, and month of year because the number of items presented over the dominant news sources varies at these times. For example, events promoted by press releases are most likely to occur during the day, Monday through Friday. The reason few press-released events occur in the evenings and on weekends is that the institutions and organization which put out the majority of these advertisements are not working at these times. By the same token, police radio monitors are more carefully scrutinized when there is more time to fill, and there is usually more police news during the evenings and on weekends.

When a story is learned about is an important consideration in whether it will presented, and how much will be said about it. How long the story is—when in the chronology of events the media begin and end their reporting—also has an effect. Most stories derived from police radio monitors have a short life span on the air—about one and a half minutes. For example, an armed robbery may be reported this way: "A liquor store at the corner of 11th and K Streets was held up at 9:00 p.m. by two young men who brandished guns to steal $100 in cash. Their getaway attempt was halted by an off-duty policeman who fired several warning shots into the air. Tonight the young men are in custody." This account will be read over film of the store, the off-duty policeman, and the cuffed suspects being led to a police car. What happens to them in jail, their feelings, bargaining for justice, and even the outcome of their case will seldom be reported.

This remains true even if suspects are mistakenly taken into custody, which occurred in Western City when two men were charged with robbing a bank. They had been seen running not far from the crime and had been stopped, questioned, and apprehended. Their faces were seen by thousands of viewers, including their families and friends, and when they were proved to have been erroneously arrested, this mistake was noted only in the middle section of the newspaper the next day; it was not mentioned in the TV newscast because, for all practical purposes, the story had ended with the initial presentation. Follow-up investigations are not as interesting as the drama of the capture.

The use of angles further illustrates the importance of when a story begins and ends. The limited time journalists have to report, write, and then present an event-as-news requires them to pre-define and simplify. I have already shown that reporters do this by treating a local event as though it were like a national news story, or by encapsulating complex political views and issues in a "horserace." When a particular angle or predefinition of an event occurs is of utmost importance for more complete news coverage. The sooner the event is transformed into an angle, the less complete the reports will be. Relatedly, the media coverage will become more infused with the event the quicker an angle is selected. It works this way because the angle is a conclusion about an event; it is a way of summarizing what is relevant to it.

The Eagleton case illustrates the point. Just after his nomination, I talked with several network correspondents about how Eagleton would be treated as a candidate. They agreed that he would be contrasted with Agnew and that this would surely help him. This view changed upon disclosure that he had a history of mental illness and had not told McGovern about his hospitalization or "shock treatments." While some journalists wanted to stick with the "new face" approach, and emphasize Eagleton's outstanding record as a senator, others began moving toward the "big question" of his honesty and stability.

Concluding Remarks

The messages which are presented to millions of viewers do not depict how the news process influences what is presented. Until newswatchers watch "defensively," and until journalists begin understanding news coverage has an impact, all stories will be incomplete and deceptive. Examining news reports in terms of who, what, where, and when permits newswatchers to speculate on how an event was selected, defined, constructed, and presented for news purposes. Such questions enable us to understand the news perspective and recontextualize the events that journalists report. Once this orientation becomes part of the cultural common sense, news reports will be more useful and less distorting.

This critical perspective does not, however, resolve the ambiguity of news. It does not tell viewers about other plausible and more complete ways of depicting events. This perception comes from the viewer's experience and analytical skills. The more viewers know about phenomena like crime, mental illness, etc., the less satisfied they will be with the news reports. However, I think that recognizing the architecture behind news images is necessary before alternative designs can be considered.

What the alternatives will be depends on what news is intended to do. If, on the one hand, it is acceptable for news reports to be shaped by organizational and other contextual influences independently of the events, then the current situation is adequate, if not optimal. On the other hand, if we want news reports to present events in context, complete with uncertainty, then present commitments to commercialism, and organizational and scheduling priorities must be reconsidered. Even these alterations will not completely "solve" the problem of the uncertainty of news reports and their significance for our lives, but they will reduce it.

Recalling the differences between network and local news illustrates how the best-intentioned and best-informed newsworkers reflect a certain perspective in their reports. National news is not constrained by the personal bonds and commitments that are found in the arenas where local news occurs. Because no one lives in a "nation" but only cities and towns, network reporters are less restrained by personal attachments to the "national" events they report. Their reports are likely to be more critical since they are about institutions, roles, and issues rather than people. These subjects are more amenable to being cast in the news perspective and examined with journalistic objectivity and professionalism than is true of local newsworkers, and especially station managers, who live with, and are friends of, those who run local affairs. To expect local reporters to do what the networks do is to deny the significance of feelings and loyalty in human affairs. Indeed, there is every indication that this practical orientation also operates at the network level; journalists who become friends with presidents and other influentials tend to be less critical of them in the public arena. In short, personal and social ties promote ingratiation which transcends professional guidelines. The focus and assessments of local journalists are likely to reflect these ties in a way not found among national reporters. This human condition clearly has a bearing on what is presented as news but I know of no way to erase it; we can only be aware of it.

My aim has been to spur construction of more truthful and complete accounts of the social world by incorporating an awareness of the news process into these events. As long as most of us see the world through news reports, we must learn to see the news for what it is. This is my hope.

METHODOLOGICAL APPENDIX

My studies of news were done through participant-observation in several settings (Altheide, 1974: 374-455). My aim was to understand how newsworkers saw their jobs, and how they actually did their work. This entailed spending a considerable amount of time with them covering and reporting news stories. In addition, I visited with them informally off the job whenever possible. I observed newsworkers in Channel B, a network affiliate, from October 1971 to September 1972. My visits were restricted to several times a week in the early months of observation, since I was preparing for my Ph.D. comprehensive examinations and had to teach part-time to support my wife and daughter. I mention these contingencies because I believe they had a bearing on my research experience. On the average, I was at Channel B about four days a week, and usually remained throughout the day or evening, depending on who I was working with. The friendships I made were helpful in my study of the national political conventions in 1972, when I was able to further examine the news teams from Channel B, as well as get a firsthand look at network TV and radio, wireservices, and newspapers.

The third setting studied was a larger, network-"owned and operated" station in Northern City. My three-day visit to this site confirmed my general understanding of TV news, although I also noted several differences.

The first three settings were the basis for my dissertation (Altheide, 1974), which was supplemented by further research. A colleague, Paul K. Rasmussen, studied the other network affiliate in Western City for more than six months, and his work clarified the broader picture of TV news in Western City.

These settings provided essential aspects of the overall news process and perspective I have analyzed in this book. I further checked out these understandings with stations in other parts of the country. I visited two stations in Washington state in December 1975, and studied specific reports by two network affiliates in Phoenix, Arizona, between January 1974 and December 1975. In brief, I have studied TV news for more than three years in various news operations in a half-dozen cities.

But quantity of experience does not guarantee validity. Only assessments of the findings and conclusions by other media researchers and journalists will uncover oversights and errors. By the same token, I do not believe that the reader should "take my word," or uncritically accept the analysis without knowing a little more about the way the study was done. While I do not believe that absolute objectivity is possible, social scientists can obtain greater degrees of confidence in findings. But this cannot be done through rhetoric or assertions of "scientific training." Nor can it be done by making claims about how extensive one's notes are. The final test of worthwhile field studies is the researcher's explication of the way the study was carried out, including oversights, errors, uncertainties, etc. The idea is to articulate how TV news was studied so that others can either see shortcomings in the data or can try to replicate the research in other settings. However, one thing seems certain to me. Field workers, like all researchers, influence the situations they encounter (Johnson, 1975). We cannot duck this problem, just as journalists cannot. But we can delineate the ways in which we have influenced the world we examined (Cicourel, 1964). This is the task of the remaining pages.

In the most general sense, objectivity means reducing or eliminating biases to let the essential phenomenon appear. This is a special problem in field research, since the investigator assumes the important data of the social world to consist of the nature and organization of subjective meanings. Even though one's understandings and definitions may be shared by members in the settings, the investigator is usually an outsider who seeks to learn how the members see their activities. This orientation precludes a researcher from assuming at the outset that he knows what is relevant or significant; he must withhold judgment until his research uncovers these important meanings. But how is a researcher to do this? On what basis should fellow scholars judge the merits of the work? Why should they even believe it? These are key issues for field researchers.

Objectivity in field research is enhanced by overcoming obstacles which prevent an investigator from learning how a setting is organized and what occurs, and, most importantly, how the members interpret it all. Locating such problems is a first step toward their resolution; we must become more sensitive to the potential sources of bias in field studies. From this vantage point, objectivity is an ongoing problem that reappears as increased knowledge of the social world, and careful monitoring of field researches, point to other problems, to potential sources of distortion. My research and that of others (cf. Johnson, 1975) have suggested certain key problems that distort what a researcher sees and understands. I believe these troublesome areas apply to most studies, and, therefore, most researchers will have to deal with them in one way or the other. Thus, I think that these problems should be regarded as contributing to one's findings. Resolving these potential roadblocks thus provides a basis for evaluating this and others' studies.

The character of my research can be presented with eight general problem areas: (1) entree; (2) approach and self-presentation; (3) trust and rapport; (4) my way of fitting in; (5) mistakes, misconceptions, and surprises; (6) data; (7) verification; (8) data collection and recording. These topics indicate the interdependence of entree, observation and understanding, and data collection and recording.

Entree

Entree, or gaining access, is a problem in all research. Not only is one's access to data affected, but the kind of information a researcher gets is also influenced. There were two kinds of entree relevant in my research: organizational or territorial, and interpersonal. Stated differently, gaining access to a setting does not guarantee meaningful access to people in that setting.

ORGANIZATIONAL ENTREE

My entree to Channel B was paved by a fellow student who worked at the station. After an initial interview with the news director, I was given guarded permission to study how the station would cover a national political event which was subsequently moved to another city. My presence in the newsroom was contingent on the news director's good will, a condition that became a problem as my research continued. My acceptance was never an accomplished fact, but was continually negotiated. On three occasions, the news director threatened to throw me out. The first confrontation occurred when I photocopied a "call sheet," the record of telephone queries from viewers. The news director had previously permitted me to photocopy a speech he had given; thus, when I could not find him to get permission to copy the call sheet, I incorrectly assumed that this seemingly harmless request would be granted. He saw me making a copy and asked what I was doing. When I told him, he ordered me to follow him to his office where he warned me about repeating this infraction. I left the newsroom for the day, feeling upset and angry, and I subsequently stole a copy of the call sheet for my files.

The second major clash occurred when I mistakenly tape recorded a conversation in a news car. I had routinely taped several cameramen and reporters, and I assumed that my first ride with a particular cameraman was also recordable since one of the reporters friendly to me was also along. I knew I was wrong when the cameraman threatened to throw me out of the car. My apologies did not prevent the cameraman from reporting the incident to the news director, who called me into his office for the second time. During this tongue-lashing, he reminded me that the event I had oroginally intended to study was no longer scheduled to occur here, and he wondered why I stayed on. He ultimately agreed to let me stay, although I never understood why.

The last confrontation occurred when I requested a letter from the station manager to help obtain credentials for the political conventions. Once again the news director called me into his office, this time to ask why I had not requested the letter from him. He refused to accept my explanation that he was out of town when I needed the letter, and that I thought a letter from the station manager might carry a bit more weight with the Republican and Democratic national committees anyway, and he said the station would not help me obtain credentials. He repeated his warning for me to stay in line, and later told one of my informants that he had brought me "down a notch or two."

My experience with the news director was typical of the experiences of other members of the newsroom. However, I also feel this experience influenced the kinds of information I obtained. For example, I was not permitted to attend editorial meetings where the news director, in opposition to "official" policy, dictated what the editorials would be, and I had to rely on reports of an informant who did attend the meetings. Nevertheless, I was constantly nervous whenever the news director was around, as were many other employees. Thus, my experience helped me understand how the newsroom operated, but it led me to adopt the *procedural rule to avoid the news director at all costs.*

I did not have these problems in other settings, although the security at the conventions complicated my study. I breached security in various ways at both conventions in order to enter the grounds, news areas—including the network booths—and the convention floor (Altheide, 1975). Once I was inside these areas, as in the other settings I studied, my presence alone gave me enough authority to be accepted, and I did not experience any of the problems characteristic of my stay at Channel B.

INTERPERSONAL ENTREE

Once organizational clearance was achieved, I still had to be accepted by the membership. I worked with all of Channel B's news staff, but established a strong relationship with only a half dozen, although no one (to my knowledge) strongly disliked me. My number of informants was affected by the overall clique structure of the newsroom, because factions were not easily bridged; to be close to members of one group seemed to mean exclusion from others.

Two of my most consistent informants were excluded from the dominant clique among cameramen, and on several occasions referred to themselves as "outsiders." Even though I made every effort to spend equal amounts of time with all news personnel,

most of my observations involved these people. Indeed, I discovered I could not work comfortably with members of both
groups. This problem is illustrated by two informants' interpretations of my diving watch and compass. Field notes on that day
reflect the dangers of wearing the symbols of the enemy among
friends.

> C.M. commented about my watch, especially the underwater compass.
> REP, said something about my having things pretty well my own way
> when I started to work here. I was a little defensive about it, insisting,
> although I was laughing, that I wasn't the least bit interested in coming
> to work here. They noted how the news director [enemy] had gauges
> all over his arm. I explained that it was a birthday gift; the cameraman
> told an intern to make a list and put me on it. . . . It raised an interest-
> ing problem about getting on with people in the setting. I'm not even
> sure that the [enemy] will like it [i.e., the watch and compass]. But,
> I like it, so what can you do? *The chances of offending somebody while
> trying to get along with another are pretty good, it seems.*

In general, I was not on equally good terms with all members
of the news staff, and did spend a disproportionate amount of
time with some. My experience with their colleagues indicated
some differences in news tasks, but on the whole, was consistent
throughout the operation.

Approach and Self-Presentation

I was defined several ways during my research. Telling people
I was a "researcher" did not make a great deal of sense to them,
at least, not in the way I intended. For one thing, most newsworkers saw research as an investigation for an exposé. On several
occasions reporters asked me when my "big exposé" would be
finished. Most approved of this, since they felt it would help get
rid of the news director and other "fools." Other newsworkers
who had some experience with sociology were uncertain about
the kind of research I was doing, because for them, research consisted of filling out questionnaires. In the words of one techni-
cian, "I am having trouble fitting this in with what I know about
sociology."

Most newsworkers believed I was trying to get a job at the

station. Even though I tried to dispel this notion whenever it arose, a few newsworkers told me as I was preparing to depart the station that I would be in a pretty good position to get a job.

This lack of agreement about my purpose had good points and bad points for the research. On the one hand, I was permitted to ask a lot of questions and to obtain elaborations of procedures and routines. On the other hand, some things that were relevant for my research were irrelevant to them. To pursue my interests in the face of their ideas about what was essential for their work often raised questions about my competence. One example was my request for permission to examine the contents of an editor's wastebasket in order to learn what he had thrown away, and the reasons for selecting some pieces over others. At first my question was misunderstood, and then disbelieved. I was told, "Nah, there's nothing in there but scrap paper." My response was to blankly nod, sort of grin, and wonder what to do next. I later found out that the contents of the wastebasket had little to do with news-work, and I must have seemed a bit odd to this man. In addition, I felt a bit conspicuous doing what I had never seen a newsworker do: pawing through someone's garbage.

Most of my requests were granted, although some people denied me more than I like to admit, especially in the early stages of re-search. Two of the denials suggest how some people avoided me. In the first case I was told that a story about an emotional blind man whose dog had been poisoned was "a little touchy." The reporter and I eventually worked together on other stories which most newsworkers would regard as even more "touchy." The other denial was by a cameraman with whom I seldom worked; it was typical of our overall relationship. I asked if I could go with him to cover crowd action at a rock-concert, and he said, "I can't do it, Dave," because of an "insurance problem": if I got hurt during any crowd action, the station could be sued.

My success at working with reporters and cameramen was also influenced by their interest in me. My first "breakthrough" came after I had spent several hours in the newsroom during my first day of observation when a cameraman volunteered to let me accompany him on a story. This man proved to be one of my more reliable informants and also a good friend; I stayed with him during my trek to Miami Beach to study the Democratic convention.

Another way I approached newsworkers grew out of one of my confrontations with the news director. When he asked how much longer I would "be around" and what I still had to do, my answers led him to demand that I give him a research schedule. This worked to my advantage since I could, when necessary, suggest to some workers, such as the assignment editor, that the news director wanted me to spend some time with him.

Trust and Rapport

The key issue here is the amount of confidence I had in informants' not giving me false information or incomplete reports. There were perhaps only six newsworkers who were quite frank with me, and, in some areas of conversation, such as the politics of the station management, fewer than this. I found that in many instances I was not told a great deal about how a worker felt because he did not tell anyone—not even his close colleagues. In other instances, this was not true; informants would tell me how they felt about the news operations and their personal affairs. I learned that trying to be in, but not part of, the interaction was a mistake. I worried about "influencing" the data and had followed a lot of conventional field-research wisdom to stay a bit aloof. That did not work in the newsroom, partly because more formal and detached interaction with one person was a sign that you were a member of the rival clique. In order to gain the trust I needed, it was essential to interact as one of the members. However, this was fraught with problems since many of the arguments newsworkers had over the issues of the day—such as race relations, welfare, poverty, and the Vietnam war—tended to divide them. I often cowered before mention of these topics for fear that I would be asked to take sides. Perhaps it was for this reason that one member described me as "so noncommunicative"—a unique assessment of my talkativeness.

My status as a researcher did not exempt me from the member's test of competence. When the situation called for evidence of shared understanding and concern about a particular matter, it was far better to risk "taking sides" than being labelled a dud. *The*

*procedural rule I used was to take cues from informants about
what I should talk about, understand, and acknowledge.* For example, the news director's activities, the conservative politics of
the station, and the arbitrary story assignments would not be
explicitly cited, especially in the newsroom. However, all members were presumed to understand this. It was common for someone to say, "You've probably been around here long enough now
to pick up some of this stuff," and "You've been around here
for a year now and you should already know. . . ." Even though
my tendency was to ask for more clarification in order to avoid
leaping to conclusions, it was evident that in some situations this
equivocal position was not legitimate.

Another brief example illustrates the significance of the members' shared understandings. One evening I mentioned to a cameraman that I was waiting to talk to the producer, a man whom
everyone felt to be incompetent. When he asked why I wanted
to see him, I said that I wanted to find out how he decided to
include certain stories and balance the show. This was a poor
choice of words. The cameraman shouted, "Balance the show!
You've been around here long enough to know better than that;
all you have to do is watch [the show]!" He then told his colleagues what I had said and questioned whether he had been
wasting his time trying to show me how news should be done.

But even this honesty and confidence were conditional. One of
my close informants incorrectly told me that he did not know
a newsman who worked for a network owned and operated station that I hoped to visit. After I selected another station to
study, the newsworker told me several weeks later that he really
knew the man quite well but did not feel as though he could just
throw me into the setting. He was concerned lest it jeopardize
the relationship he had with this network employee and friend.

My Way of Fitting In

The quality of information a researcher obtains in a setting will
depend on how the members define him. How a researcher fits,
or is made to "belong," in a setting will influence whether his
presence is natural or disruptive. I learned to let the members
define me. I mentioned that many newsworkers at Channel B

believed I was trying to get a job by "hanging around." This was a natural category, since "interns" would periodically do volunteer work in the newsroom in order to learn more about news, obtain letters of recommendation for future jobs, and in some cases, get a job at the station if a position opened up.

I learned more about Channel B's news on assignments with crews than from staying around the station. The news director was one reason: I did not want to be wherever he was, and he was usually at the station. I did learn about editing and other production techniques at the station, and did have some good interviews, but my presence was not as natural as it was with some reporters and cameramen. I not only observed their work, I also helped them. Packing equipment, plugging in lights, and solving logistics problems like keeping children away from the camera enabled me to contribute to their work but also fill a niche for natural observation. I was not in the way and was soon taken for granted. A few reporters and cameramen even began including me as part of their "crew."

I did not fully understand the reasons for this until several months into my research. Channel B used only a reporter and a cameraman to cover stories. Unlike network operations, which had an assistant cameraman, a lighting man, or electrician, and a sound man, Channel B's setup was such that camera operators had to do all of this. Most did it quite well and had established routines to solve these practical tasks, but my presence permitted several to make me into a "sound man" or an "electrician." They enjoyed it, I gained further access to their activities and perspectives, and they became, in their words, "just like the network boys."

My involvement with the workers in these settings provided a lot of time for conversation and reflection as we traveled to and from the station, and from one story to another. Our contact made us friends and established a firm basis for conversations in various parts of the station, motel rooms, and bars. Moreover, this experience provided more complete understanding that proved invaluable in adjusting to new situations in the other settings I studied. I helped set up lights and tripods, and packed gear with confidence throughout the rest of my research adventure.

Mistakes, Misconceptions, and Surprises

Unlike most research manuals, which caution researchers against making mistakes, I find that mistakes are inevitable. Not to make mistakes implies that the researcher already understands the meanings, perspectives, and problems of those he studies, and since these are what field researchers seek to uncover, it is likely that they will make a variety of errors during the research journey to the world their subjects inhabit. Conversely, the researcher will make fewer mistakes as he becomes more familiar with the setting. More importantly, recognizing that mistakes have been made is a test of how much the researcher is learning. The same is true with misconceptions and surprises. I used examples of each to indicate my progress in learning about the perspective of news-workers. In short, mistakes should be welcomed and not avoided or made to disappear by casting them out of one's field notes.

My experience with the "show order," or the schedule of stories, commercials, etc., illustrates this. One problem I had was to act like a researcher. I grabbed practically the first thing that struck me as data—a copy of a "show order." While I later used this to illustrate how news sources interact with scheduling demands, I did not know about that at the time. I began to conjecture about all sorts of things I could do with it. An excerpt from my field notes during my first week of observation illustrates this.

It might be interesting to see if some reporters get more time on the air. It should be pretty easy to do with the show time sheets over a period of time to see if there are any gross discrepancies and come up with some sort of an informal kind of order. I am not sure, it is just a thought.

I thoroughly studied this document and noted several days later:

When I first got here this afternoon [Reporter] came up to me and asked me what I was doing and I told her I was looking for information and was trying to figure out if there was any difference between the noon news and the nightly news. She said there was a difference in format, and I said that I knew that, but I was wondering about the content, and I asked her if there was any sports [on the noon news]. She said there was.

I could have answered my own question by simply watching the noon news. That approach did not seem sensible given my preoccupation with the "show order" as a document for newswork before I understood in any precise way exactly what it did in fact document. In other words, I was looking for information but was unable to recognize it. I think that part of this display of hyper-research consciousness can be attributed to the problems of entree, and what I thought the members expected of a researcher. Another important parameter was my coming to grips with the research activity. This is again suggested by field notes during the first month of research.

> I went through the show order and added up the amount of news time —including sports and weather—that is spent on stories, that is, reporting stories in the news. . . . I also went through and wrote down where I had them, the names of those people who had either written or filmed those stories. And, obviously, I could have gotten that from the show order and not transferred it to another sheet of paper, but *it did give me something to do.* And I was able *to focus on something . . . which I am finding is kind of important to do.*

These items (and others) struck me as relevant to my research upon entering the setting; having only these impressions to pursue an analysis of the members' role in the news scene meant that I started with strange, and often inaccurate, interpretations of these features. Most importantly, however, it was a start. But "beginning" will always produce mistakes. Learning the utility and applicability of these notions served to reorient my focus and tended to highlight other relevant dimensions. The point is not merely that I made mistakes, but that the recognition of these erroneous interpretations paved the way to an optimum understanding.

This problem stems from the researcher's inclination to "take charge" and get on with the study even before he is certain what to study. Stated differently, one can do a study about anything, but if that study is claimed to reflect the members' understanding, then the researcher has an obligation to guard against the tendency to go off in any direction in order to complete the research. *My ad hoc strategy was to defocus the details of the study until my ex-*

perience illuminated what was relevant to newswork. In practical terms, this meant that I could not question everything that happened, nor dissect specific acts, until I understood more about the context in which they occurred. I did my superficial best until I encountered puzzling situations which did not make sense according to my slowly accumulating wisdom about what I felt to be important.

Competence played a part in my research in at least two ways. First, I occasionally had to feign understanding when I was really ignorant in order to not further disrupt the course of action. This was true of technical matters—for example, someone explaining that film was "forced" in order to make underexposed film much darket. Even though I only vaguely understood the term, I knew that an interruption to ask "what do you mean by force?" would have been very disruptive. At other times, newsmen would be discussing how a colleague had "screwed up" the evening film order so that the A roll and B roll were not compatible. My early days in the setting had simply not provided enough experience with this terminology for me to quickly visualize what they were talking about. Nevertheless, in not understanding what was being said, I learned what to focus on.

Surprises, like mistakes and misconceptions, suggest what the researcher has overlooked. The field worker's problem is not to just *learn* how the members look at their tasks, but to also *delineate* the components of their perspective. This requires an assessment of what the researcher has learned. In the course of my research, I took for granted many things which could not be treated as data until their significance was topicalized. For example, one evening I gave a tour of the newsroom to a colleague who was anticipating a study of Channel A. He picked up a stopwatch and asked me what they were used for. I had not mentioned stopwatches in my notes even though I had seen them used daily for timing stories and editing procedures. I was surprised at how I had overlooked this very essential ingredient of television news—time. It had been as much a part of my daily round as the reporters who used the watches.

Data

My findings about the news process are derived from observation, conversations, interviews, documents, newscasts, and natural experiments. But one's data depend on an awareness of what is important for the research purpose. Relatedly, openness to the various activities can suggest "data gaps." Thus, data and observations are related; a researcher learns from his experience, but also focuses on what he believes to be important.

I used different types of data, but relied on some more than others. Written and spoken words helped clarify my understanding of the news process, but were not the sole basis. Indeed, I found that to rely on spoken messages was to miss a lot of the important nuances, and unstated aspects of the news setting. For example, some members would not explicitly state their disagreements with the news director and station management. Others refrained from describing "how bad things are," although any competent member was expected to know it. Some workers would indicate their feelings with facial expressions, or say simply, "You know what I mean." And one member croaked like a frog when given certain assignments. These utterances made sense to me because of the context in which they occurred.

The context also made written documents meaningful as data. For example, the "show orders" indicated who the writer, cameraman, and other "talent" were on a given story. When I had no reason to assume that the "show order" distorted who originated a report, it was a useful source of data for getting a broad picture of how many stories some people were involved with, and whether or not some people received a disproportionate amount of "good stories." But the show order was less useful for editorials, since the editorial researcher would be given "credit" for the station's position and the actual writing, when I knew from other experience that the news director was responsible for both. Thus, my experience taught me what data were relevant to the news process, and it also taught me which sources were more valid. *The rule of thumb I followed was to give more credence to something I had seen or heard.*

Criticism, humor, and accidents became data for clarifying the news perspective after I understood the routines and intricacies of newswork. What people were criticized for suggested standards of performance that I felt to be important, but was often unsure of. Once a coworker would be "ranked" by his colleagues, I could then ask for more specific information, such as "You mean, he doesn't take the time to light the scene properly?" Much the same was true with humor and accidents. Understanding what news-workers laughed about, and how some topics were unique to their work, further clarified their perspective.

"Accidents" appeared as if by chance, because I did not under-stand their place in the news process. For example, I wondered about the use of TV news by "outside" groups who lacked the official public relations sponsorship, or inside contacts with people like the mayor and chief of police. I felt I would not be able to get at this part of the news scene until I pursued another study.

While sitting in the newsroom, I met one of the city's top political activists. Our conversations about his reason for being at the station, and the problems of gaining access to news, illumi-nated another side of the news perspective. Another "accident" occurred as I left the mayor's office after an interview. A secretary told the reporter to say "Hi" to her friend at Channel B, the news director. The cameraman added that the news director was down there quite a lot. My impression of this development is contained in my notes for the day.

> One of the more interesting aspects of the day's work is that I was assuming that the place to find out about their editorial policy and certain related station-city hall connections was to hang around the station more and pick brains by some sort of interview if necessary. I felt this might be all I have since getting into the actual decision-making area would be tough since I have been barred from the editorial meet-ings. . . . The interesting thing is that I was somewhat wrong: there is a lot to be learned about the station's ties with the mayor . . . by staying in the field where such ties are made real [through news stories].

Verification

I verified what I saw, heard, and understood in order to avoid letting mere impressions or exceptional cases be mistaken for "the way it is." This process involved looking into other affiliate stations, a network owned and operated station, and some aspects of network news. I am satisfied that my findings reflect the similarities and differences relevant to organized newswork and the news perspective.

I verified what had actually occurred by checking a finding in as many ways as were warrented by my involvement in the setting. This was easier to do with Channel B reports than with the network stories I examined.

My procedure was to cross-check what I saw with what I heard. In this way, I could evaluate the trustworthiness of informants, as well as their attention to detail. If a discrepancy occurred, I would check further. However, newsworkers in general, and especially my best informants, were not accustomed to being grilled about things they regarded as trivial or important. One cameraman answered an inquiry about editing techniques with, "Look, I have already told you. . . ." I had to abandon an interview with the editorial researcher when he accused me of "pumping" him. Others would tell me things simply because I had asked and not because they knew a great deal about them.

This experience led me to eavesdrop on conversations whenever I could. If one worker told another something I had been told, observed, or surmised, then I had increased confidence that I understood how the person saw things. An anchorman had told me that he detested the current format and that he felt the news director, producer, and assignment editor were inept. One evening I heard him whisper the same thing to one of his friends. This buttressed my confidence that he was not just telling me a story.

Another example of verifying my impressions involved the two cameramen who were also reserve police officers. I had been told that they were "pro-police" in their work and that they often got their roles confused, I had heard them talk a lot about police practices, exercises, "busts," and organizational problems, and saw the exceptional array of radio monitors they had purchased for their cars. I also heard a reporter describe a situation when one man put down his camera and help police move patrol cars into position to quell a disturbance at a rock concert. But I still wanted more. An understanding of the priorities of cameramen provided this additional information. It was common practice for cameramen to save a few frames of film they were fond of, or planned to use as slides. (For examples, one informant had a collection of shots of sunsets, and surfers. Another liked cloud formations.) But the reserve police officers saved footage of police officials, sheriff's deputies, the buildings, jail signs, and some suspects. By itself this information would hardly qualify as "data," but it did support the other information I had about these workers being sympathetic to police practices. Nevertheless, my understanding of their police connections and the impact this may have had on news practices was limited to second-hand information and inferences, rather than dircct involvement with, say, a police official asking them to "give him a break." The same was true with the connection among the mayor, the news director, and the station manager. These people were far too shrewd to let me accompany them to their luncheons, join them for cocktails, or fill me in about their connection. The best I could do was rely on more filtered understandings. Thus, my statements about these influences on the news process must be taken as suggestive, and perhaps supportive of other research, but certainly not exhaustive. Only researchers with direct access to these settings will be able to provide sounder information.

I was able to demonstrate that the news director censored the "feedback" some members received from the audience. The editorial researcher sometimes doubled as the morning anchorman. He shared this task with a reporter for one week. Both men felt they had been getting only negative comments from the news director, although they had reason to believe that some viewers had been supportive. I agreed to have two of my friends write letters supporting their efforts, and they agreed to tell me what happened. The letters were sent, but were never received. This "natural experiment" confirmed their suspicions about the news director's conduct and gave me more confidence that their understanding about this and other matters could be taken seriously. This was the only time that I was explicitly involved in creating data for my study.

It is one thing to check if the news director censors mail, but it is something else to examine my understanding of the members' perspective. This is always the more ambitious task. I used humor to this end:

C.M. said the station would be getting a new camera which the chief photographer would get. Another cameraman would get his old one. He facetiously added that the chief photographer really needs new equipment. I added that you need good stuff when you shoot those sportscasters' luncheons. He agreed. I definitely understood why he felt the chief photographer didn't need equipment; I know what he covers, i.e., those luncheons.

Laughing together demonstrates a shared stock of knowledge and should be essential data for all fieldwork.

Data Collection and Recording

Data collection and data recording are not the same thing. Data recording is transforming conversations, observations, feelings, and meanings into documents such as audio recordings, notes, or materials to be understood by others outside the setting who sympathetically entertain the researcher's presentation of reality through the always unwittingly bold medium of scientific discourse. The data collected are essential to the data recorded, which are necessarily an incomplete representation of the researcher's experience. A researcher always knows more than he has recorded but hopes that the recordings do him justice before a sympathetic community of scholars.

I collected data by observing, participating, and talking with newsworkers in various situations. These materials would then be recorded by taking brief notes. This would be done, in most cases, away from newsworkers. I would then use these notes as reminders for "debriefing" into a tape recorder as I drove home, and would fill in the day's events during the next few days. Most of the day's recorded notes would then be transcribed within a few days of their collection.

I used a tape recorder mainly for debriefing, although I also used it for recording in the setting. In this way, data collection and data recording were combined. However, I found that, with some exceptions, the recorder disrupted the naturalness of the conversation. This occurred during a talk I was having with an anchorman who was making a documentary about alcoholism. His fascinating comments about using actors to play alcoholics because "real alcoholics talk too much," prompted me to ask him if he would mind if I got my recorder. When I turned it on, he cleared his throat and began lecturing me on the magnitude of alcoholism in Western City, never returning to the original topic.

In other situations the recorder did not disrupt the event. One reporter's explanation about how he "reduced" an interview was recorded without distortion. I know this to be true since I had watched him reduce other interviews in the same way. A few cameramen and reporters permitted me to routinely record their work and assessments of the news scene, while others, like the cameraman who threatened to throw me out of the car, did not approve. However, the recorder did have a situated significance for all workers.

I tried to resolve the impact of the recorder and still maintain access to it when warranted by using it less obtrusively, carrying it in a jacket pocket. This infrequently involved recording in which the speakers were unaware that the machine was on, but most of the time I would say, "Hold it, I would like to get this," then hit the button, and add, "Go ahead." However, I am now convinced that I did not fully understand the significance of the recorder to all persons involved. One informant's comments over a period of several months suggest that even those most tolerant of electronic recording had a sense about the meaning of "going on record." At one point I jotted in my notes, "[Cameraman] and I are really getting along pretty well. He seems to be pretty spontaneous with me and doesn't seem to mind the recorder." While we were eating lunch several weeks later, his comments were prefaced with "don't record this stuff." I told him I did not have my recorder with me, but I was puzzled by the precautions. A few weeks later, he asked if I lost my recorder, adding that he hadn't seen it lately. I wondered if he was suspicious. Approximately one month later he explained to a new reporter what I was doing at the station. My field notes depict my consternation at what followed.

> C.M. said that I used to have a little tape recorder which I would put in my pocket and nobody could see that I was recording. I laughed, sort of nervously, for obvious reasons [e.g., I had been warned about "secret recording" by the news director] and said that I had never done that. The cameraman's point, however, was that I didn't really make

sense out of "these crazy guys." It was funny because he was partially right.

A few hours later, we were talking when another informant asked what I had been doing. Before I could answer, the new reporter said that I "had been sneaking around in back rooms talking into my recorder about those guys at Channel B." My nervous laughter and my upset stomach indicated that I was reassessing my decision to use the recorder at all. Nevertheless, I felt that the cameraman-informant never manufactured information of played to the recorder. For one thing, he never curtailed his cursing or modified his hostile comments about the management of the newsroom.

In sum, the recorder was as much of a hindrance as a help in gaining a full understanding of newswork. I quickly abandoned any hope of obtaining literal recordings of what had occurred and used it mostly for debriefing. I also have no reason to suspect that my note-taking influenced the ongoing activities.

Concluding Remarks

My experience with entree, observation and understanding, and data collection and recording, indicates that they are not distinct research endeavors. Just as I could not observe what was relevant to the news process until a certain amount of understanding had occurred, I could not collect and record significant data without an awareness of how one datum fit with others. In the process I may have missed something.

Finally, I have dealt with some of the major sources of bias in my study. If bias in fieldwork is conceived as any interference with the researcher's understanding of the members' meanings and perspectives, then each of the topics I have dealt with is central to questions of objectivity in field research. Only honest appraisals of the research experience, shortcomings, and uncertainties will provide more information to add to the list of central research problems and ways to resolve them.

REFERENCES

ADAMS, S. (1975) "Cover-up: Playing war with numbers." Harpers (May): 41-44, 62-73.

ALTHEIDE, D. L. (1974) "The News Scene." Ph.D. dissertation, University of California, San Diego.

——— (1975) "The irony of security." Urban Life (July): 179-196.

——— and P. K. RASMUSSEN (1976) "Becoming news: A study of two newsrooms." Sociology of Work and Occupations: An International Journal (May).

American Research Bureau (1971) "Description of methodology." New York: American Research Bureau.

ANDERSON, J. (1974) The Anderson Papers. New York: Ballantine.

BARRETT, M. (ed.) (1973) The Politics of Broadcasting. New York: Thomas Y. Crowell.

BECHTEL, R. B., R. AKERS, and C. ACHELPOHL (1972) "Correlates Between Observed Behavior and Questionnaire Responses on Television Viewing," pp. 257-273 in Eli A. Rubinstein, George A. Comstock, and John P. Murray (eds.) Television and Social Behavior: Television in Day-to-Day Life: Patterns of Use. Washington, D.C.: U.S. Government Printing Office.

BERNSTEIN, C. and B. WOODWARD (1974) All the President's Men. New York: Warner.

BOORSTIN, D. (1961) The Image. New York: Atheneum.

BREED, W. (1955) "Social control in the newsroom." Social Forces 33 (May): 326-335.

BURNS, T. (1969) "Public service and private world," pp. 53-74 in Paul Halmos (ed.) "The Sociology of Mass-Media Communicators." Sociological Review Monograph, No. 13 (January).

CHASE, I. H. (1973) "An affair to remember." Mental Health 57 (Summer): 8-11.

CICOUREL, A. V. (1964) Method and Measurement in Sociology. New York: Free Press.

COHEN, S. and J. YOUNG (eds.) (1973) The Manufacture of News. Beverly Hills, Calif.: Sage.

CROUSE, T. (1972) The Boys on the Bus. New York: Ballantine.

DANZGER, M. H. (1975) "Validating conflict data." American Sociological Review 40 (October): 570-584.

DeFLEUR, M. (1970) Theories of Mass Communication. New York: David McKay.

DOUGLAS, J. D. (1970) "Understanding Everyday Life," pp. 3-44 in Jack D. Douglas (ed.) Understanding Everyday Life. Chicago: Aldine.

——— and J. M. JOHNSON (eds.) (1976) Existential Sociology. New York: Cambridge University Press.

EFRON, E. (1971) The News Twisters. Los Angeles: Nash.

ELLIOTT, P. (1972) The Making of a Television Series. London: Constable.

EPSTEIN, E. J. (1973) *News from Nowhere.* New York: Random House.
EVANS, R. I. (1969) "How good are the ratings?" National Association of Educational Broadcasters (January-February): 39-50.
FANG, I. (1968) *Television News.* New York: Hasting House.
FERGUSON, J. R. (1972) "Network Coverage of the Major Democratic Candidates," pp. 13-89 in R. Emmett Tyrrell, Jr. (ed.) *Report of Network News Treatment of the 1972 Democratic Presidential Candidates.* Bloomington, Ind.: The Alternative Educational Foundation, Inc.
FRIENDLY, F. W. (1967) *Due to Circumstances Beyond Our Control.* New York: Vintage.
GIEBER, W. (1960) "How the 'gatekeepers' view local civil liberties news." Journalism Quarterly 37: 199-205.
——— (1961) "Two communicators of the news: A study of the roles of sources and reporters." Social Forces 39: 76-83.
——— and W. JOHNSON (1961) "The city hall beat: A study of reporter and source roles." Journalism Quarterly 38: 289-297.
HALBERSTAM, D. (1974) "Press and prejudice: How our last three presidents got the newsmen they deserved." Esquire (April): 109-114, 227-231.
——— (1976) "CBS: The power and the profits, parts I and II." Atlantic (January): 33-71; (February): 52-91.
HUBBARD, J. C., M. L. DeFLEUR, and L. B. DeFLEUR (1975) "Mass media influence on public conceptions of social problems." Social Problems 23 (October): 22-35.
HUGHES, H. M. (1940) *News and the Human Interest Story.* Chicago: University of Chicago Press.
IRWIN, W. (1911) "The American newspaper." Colliers Weekly 46 (January, 21): 15-18.
JOHNSON, J. M. (1975) *Doing Field Research.* New York: Free Press.
KLAPP, O. (1972) *Currents of Unrest.* New York: Holt, Rinehart & Winston.
KNAPPMAN, E. W. (1973) *Watergate and the White House: June, 1972-July, 1973.* New York: Facts on File.
LEWIN, K. (1949) "Channels of group life." Human Relations 1: 143-153.
LIPPMAN, W. (1922) *Public Opinion.* New York: Free Press.
LYMAN, S. M. and M. B. SCOTT (1970) *A Sociology of the Absurd.* New York: Appleton-Century-Crofts.
LYMAN, S. M. (1975) "Legitimacy and consensus in Lipset's America: From Washington to Watergate." Social Research 42 (Winter): 729-759.
McCOMBS, M. G. and D. L. SHAW (1972) "The agenda setting function of mass media." Public Opinion Quarterly 36 (Summer): 176-187.
McLUHAN, M. (1960) *Explorations in Communication.* (with E. S. Carpenter) Boston: Beacon Press.
——— (1962) *The Gutenberg Galaxy: The Making of Typographical Man.* Toronto: University of Toronto Press.
——— (1964) *Understanding Media: The Extensions of Man.* New York: McGraw-Hill.
——— (1967) *The Medium is the Massage: An Inventory of Effects.* (with Quentin Fiore) New York: Random House.
McQUAIL, D. (1969) *Towards a Sociology of Mass Communications.* London: Collier-Macmillan.
MALLOY, M. T. (1975) "Journalistic ethics: A rainbow of gray." National Observer (July 26).
MANKIEWICZ, F. (1975) *U.S. v. Richard M. Nixon.* New York: Quadrangle.
MARCUSE, H. (1964) *One-Dimensional Man.* Boston: Beacon Press.

MOLOTCH, H. and M. LESTER (1974) "News as purposive behavior." American Sociological Review 39 (February): 101-112.

MUELLER, C. (1973) *The Politics of Communication.* New York: Oxford University Press.

New York Times Staff (1973) *The White House Transcripts.* New York: Bantam Books. (Originally published by the Government Printing Office, Washington, D.C.)

NIELSEN, A. C. (1964) "What the ratings really mean." Los Angeles: A. C. Nielsen Co.

NUNNALLY, J. C., Jr. (1961) *Popular Conceptions of Mental Health.* New York: Holt, Rinehart & Wisnton.

PARK, R. E. (1923) "Natural history of the newspaper." American Journal of Sociology 29 (November): 80-98.

——— (1940) "News as a form of knowledge." American Journal of Sociology 45 (March): 669-686.

Roper Organization (1971) "An Extended View of Public Attitudes Toward Television and Other Mass Media." New York: Television Information Office.

ROSHCO, B. (1973) *Newsmaking.* Chicago: University of Chicago Press.

ROSTEN, L. (1937) *The Washington Correspondents.* New York: Harcourt, Brace.

SCHEFF, T. (1966) *Being Mentally Ill.* Chicago: Aldine.

——— (ed.) (1967) *Mental Illness and Social Processes.* New York: Harper & Row.

——— (1974) "The labelling theory of mental illness." American Sociological Review 39 (June): 444-452.

SCHLESINGER, A. M., Jr. (1973) *The Imperial Presidency.* Boston: Houghton Mifflin.

SCHUTZ, A. (1967) *The Phenomenology of the Social World.* (translated by G. Walsh and F. Lehnert.) Evanston, Ill.: Northwestern University Press.

SHIBUTANI, T. (1966) *Improvised News: A Sociological Study of Rumor.* Indianapolis: Bobbs-Merrill.

SIGAL, L. V. (1973) *Reporters and Officials.* Lexington, Mass.: D. C. Heath.

SKORNIA, H. (1965) *Television and Society.* New York: McGraw-Hill.

SORENSON, T. C. (1965) *Kennedy.* New York: Harper & Row.

SZASZ, T. (1961) *The Myth of Mental Illness: Foundations of a Theory of Personal Conduct.* New York: Hoeber-Harper.

——— (1970) *Ideology and Insanity.* Garden City, N.Y.: Doubleday.

TANNENBAUM, P. (1963) "Communication of science information." Science 140 (May): 579-583.

TUCHMAN, G. (1969) "News, the Newsman's Reality," Ph.D. dissertation, Brandeis University.

——— (1972) "Objectivity as strategic ritual." American Journal of Sociology 77 (January): 660-679.

——— (1973) "Making news by doing work: Routinizing the unexpected." American Journal of Sociology 79 (July): 110-131.

——— (ed.) (1974) *The TV Establishment.* Englewood Cliffs, N.H': Prentice-Hall.

TUNSTALL, J. (1972) "New Organization Goals and Specialist Newsgathering Journalists," pp. 259-280 in Denis McQuail (ed.) *Sociology of Mass Communications.* Middlesex, England: Penguin.

VIDICH, A. J. (1975) "Political legitimacy in bureaucratic society: An analysis of Watergate." Social Research 42 (Winter): 778-814.

WEAVER, P. (1972) "Is television news biased?" Public Interest 26 (Winter): 57-74.

WHITE, D. M. (1950) "The gatekeeper: A case study in the selection of news." Journalism Quarterly 27 (Fall): 383-390.

WHITE, T. (1973) *The Making of the President, 1972.* New York: Bantam Books.

WHITE, T. (1975) *Breach of Faith: The Fall of Richard M. Nixon.* New York: Quadrangle.

WILDE, W. (1969) "Official News: Decision Making in a Metropolitan Newspaper." Ph.D. dissertation, Northwestern University.

WOLF, F. (1972) *Television Programming for News and Public Affairs.* New York: Praeger.

YOUNG, J. (1973) "The Amplification of Drug Use," pp. 350-359 in Stanley Cohen and Jock Young (ed.) *The Manufacture of News.* Beverly Hills, Calif.: Sage.

ABOUT THE AUTHOR

DAVID L. ALTHEIDE is Assistant Professor of Sociology at Arizona State University in Tempe, Arizona. He has been interested in network and local news operations for the past three or four years, and his Ph.D. dissertation was entitled "The News Scene" (University of California, San Diego, 1974). He is also the author (with Paul Rasmussen) of "Becoming News: A Study of Two Newsrooms," published in the journal SOCIOLOGY OF WORK AND OCCUPATIONS (May 1976). His other publications include "The Irony of Security," published in 1975 in the journal URBAN LIFE. During production of this book, he also produced Tod Carl Altheide, 6 lbs., 11 ozs.

NOTES

NOTES

NOTES